Quantitative Data Analysis with SPSS Release 10 for Windows

The latest edition of this best-selling textbook has been completely updated to accommodate the needs of users of SPSS Release 10 for Windows.

As with previous editions, Alan Bryman and Duncan Cramer provide a non-technical approach to quantitative data analysis and a user-friendly introduction to the widely used SPSS for Windows. They assume no previous familiarity with either statistics or computing, but take readers step-by-step through techniques, including:

- correlation
- simple and multiple regression
- multivariate analysis of variance and covariance
- factor analysis

They also include a comprehensive range of exercises for further practice and cover issues such as sampling, statistical significance, conceptualisation and measurement and the selection of appropriate tests.

The datasets used in *Quantitative Data Analysis with SPSS Release 10 for Windows* are available via the Internet at:

http://www.routledge.com/textbooks/titles/quant10.html

Alan Bryman and **Duncan Cramer** both teach at Loughborough University and have written several books on statistical analysis with SPSS and with Minitab.

Quantitative Data Analysis with SPSS Release 10 for Windows

A guide for social scientists

Alan Bryman and Duncan Cramer

First published 2001 by Routledge
27 Church Road, Hove, East Sussex BN3 2FA

Simultaneously published in the USA and Canada
by Taylor & Francis Inc
325 Chestnut Street, Suite 800, Philadelphia, PA 19106

Routledge is an imprint of the Taylor & Francis Group

© 2001 Routledge

Typeset in Times by Regent Typesetting, London
Printed and bound in Great Britain by Biddles Ltd, Guildford and
King's Lynn

British Library Cataloguing in Publication Data
A catalogue record for this book is available from the British
Library

Library of Congress Cataloging in Publication Data
Bryman, Alan.
    Quantitative data analysis with SPSS Release 10 for Windows :
a guide for social scientists / Alan Bryman and Duncan Cramer.
-- [Completely updated ed.]
        p. cm.
    Includes bibliographical references and index.
    1. SPSS for Windows. 2. Social sciences--Statistical methods--
Computer programs. I. Cramer, Duncan, 1948- II. Title.

    HA32 .B796 2001
    300'.285'5369--dc21
                                                    00-056032

ISBN 0-415-24399-8 (hbk)
ISBN 0-415-24400-5 (pbk)

For Sue, Sarah and Stella

Contents

Figures

Boxes

Tables

Preface

In this book, we introduce readers to the main techniques of statistical analysis employed by psychologists and sociologists. However, we do not see the book as a standard introduction to statistics. We see it as distinctively different because we are not concerned to introduce the often complex formulae that underlie the statistical methods covered. Students often find these formulae and the calculations that are associated with them extremely daunting, especially when their background in mathematics is weak. Moreover, in these days of powerful computers and packages of statistical programs, it seems gratuitous to put students through the anxiety of confronting complex calculations when machines can perform the bulk of the work. Indeed, most practitioners employ statistical packages that are run on computers to perform their calculations, so there seems little purpose in treating formulae and their application as a *rite de passage* for social scientists. Moreover, few students would come to understand fully the rationale for the formulae that they would need to learn. Indeed, we prefer the term 'quantitative data analysis' to 'statistics' because of the adverse image that the latter term has in the minds of many prospective readers.

In view of the widespread availability of statistical packages and computers, we feel that the two areas which students need to get to grips with are how to decide which statistical procedures are suitable for which purpose and how to interpret the ensuing results. We try to emphasise these two elements in this book.

In addition, the student needs to get to know how to operate the computer and in particular how to use the computer software needed to perform the statistical procedures described in this book. To this end, we introduce students to what is probably the most widely used suite of programs for statistical analysis in the social sciences – the Statistical Package for the Social Sciences (SPSS). This package was first developed in the 1960s and was the first major attempt to provide software for the social scientist. It has since undergone numerous revisions and refinements. The first two editions of this book (Bryman and Cramer, 1990, 1994) dealt with versions of SPSS that were designed for mainframe computers or for the Microsoft operating system MS-DOS. A few years ago, a version of SPSS was developed to operate within the widely used Microsoft Windows environment. This too has undergone a number of revisions. The next edition of this book

(Bryman and Cramer, 1997) was concerned with Release 6 for Windows which was designed for Microsoft Windows 3.11. After the introduction of Windows 95, a new release of SPSS (Release 7) was designed to run on this operating system. The latest version for Windows 95 is Release 10. The present book describes the use of Release 10, which we shall refer to as SPSS for short unless otherwise indicated. The use of Releases 8 and 9 is described in the previous edition of this book (Bryman and Cramer, 1999).

In order to distinguish methods of quantitative data analysis from SPSS commands, the latter are always in **bold**. We also present some data that students can work on and the names of the variables are also in bold (for example, **income**). The data sets can be copied from the Routledge website on the Internet at the following address: http://www.routledge.com/textbooks/quant10.html.

There are exercises at the end of each chapter and the answers are provided for all exercises at the end of the book. We hope that students and instructors alike find these useful; they can easily be adapted to provide further exercises.

The case for combining methods of quantitative data analysis used by both psychologists and sociologists in part derives from our belief that the requirements of students of the two subjects often overlap substantially. None the less, instructors can omit particular techniques as they wish.

We wish to thank David Stonestreet, formerly of Routledge, for his support of the earlier editions of this book and our current editor Vivien Ward for her support of the present book. We also wish to thank Louis Cohen, Max Hunt and Tony Westaway for reading the manuscript for the first edition of this book and for making useful suggestions for improvement. We accept that they cannot be held liable for any errors in that or the present edition. Such errors are entirely of our own making, though we shall undoubtedly blame each other for them.

ALAN BRYMAN AND DUNCAN CRAMER
Loughborough University

Chapter 1

Data analysis and the research process

This book largely covers the field that is generally referred to as 'statistics', but as our Preface has sought to establish, we have departed in a number of respects from the way in which this subject is conventionally taught to under- and post-graduates. In particular, our preferences are for integrating data analysis with computing skills and for not burdening the student with formulae. These predilections constitute a departure from many, if not most, treatments of this subject. We prefer the term 'quantitative data analysis' because the emphasis is on the understanding and analysis of data rather than on the precise nature of the statistical techniques themselves.

Why should social science students have to study quantitative data analysis, especially at a time when qualitative research is coming increasingly to the fore (Bryman, 1988a)? After all, everyone has heard of the ways in which statistical materials can be distorted, as indicated by Disraeli's often-quoted dictum: 'There are lies, damn lies and statistics.' Why should serious researchers and students be prepared to get involved in such a potentially unworthy activity? If we take the first issue – why should social science students study quantitative data analysis – it is necessary to remember that an extremely large proportion of the empirical research undertaken by social scientists is designed to generate or draws upon quantitative data. In order to be able to appreciate the kinds of analyses that are conducted in relation to such data and possibly to analyse their own data (especially since many students are required to carry out projects), an acquaintance with the appropriate methods of analysis is highly desirable for social science students. Further, although qualitative research has quite properly become a prominent strategy in sociology and some other areas of the social sciences, it is by no means as pervasive as quantitative research, and in any case many writers recognise that there is much to be gained from a fusion of the two research traditions (Bryman, 1988a).

On the question of the ability of statisticians to distort the analyses that they carry out, the prospects for which are substantially enhanced in many people's eyes by books with such disconcerting titles as *How to Lie with Statistics* (Huff, 1973), it should be recognised that an understanding of the techniques to be covered in our book will greatly enhance the ability to see through the misrepresentations about which many people are concerned. Indeed, the inculcation of a sceptical appreciation of quantitative data analysis is beneficial in the light of the pervasive use of statistical data in everyday life. We are deluged with such data in the form of the results of opinion polls, market research findings, attitude surveys, health and crime statistics, and so on. An awareness of quantitative data analysis greatly enhances the ability to recognise faulty conclusions or potentially biased manipulations of the information. There is even a fair chance that a substantial proportion of the readers of this book will get jobs in which at some point they will have to think about the question of how to analyse and present statistical material. Moreover, quantitative data analysis does not comprise a mechanical application of predetermined techniques by statisticians and others; it is a subject with its own controversies and debates, just like the social sciences themselves. Some of these areas of controversy will be brought to the reader's attention where appropriate.

QUANTITATIVE DATA ANALYSIS AND THE RESEARCH PROCESS

In this section, the way in which quantitative data analysis fits into the research process – specifically the process of quantitative research – will be explored. As we shall see, the area covered by this book does not solely address the question of how to deal with quantitative data, since it is also concerned with other aspects of the research process that impinge on data analysis.

Figure 1.1 provides an illustration of the chief steps in the process of quantitative research. Although there are grounds for doubting whether research always conforms to a neat linear sequence (Bryman, 1988a, 1988b), the components depicted in Figure 1.1 provide a useful model. The following stages are delineated by the model.

Theory

The starting point for the process is a theoretical domain. Theories in the social sciences can vary between abstract general approaches (such as functionalism) and fairly low-level theories to explain specific phenomena (such as voting behaviour, delinquency, aggressiveness). By and large, the theories that are most likely to receive direct empirical attention are those which are at a fairly low level of generality. Merton (1967) referred to these as theories of the middle range, to denote theories that stood between general, abstract theories and empirical findings. Thus, Hirschi (1969), for example, formulated a 'control theory' of juvenile delinquency which proposes that delinquent acts are more likely to occur when the child's bonds to society are breached. This theory in large part derived from other theories and also from research findings relating to juvenile delinquency.

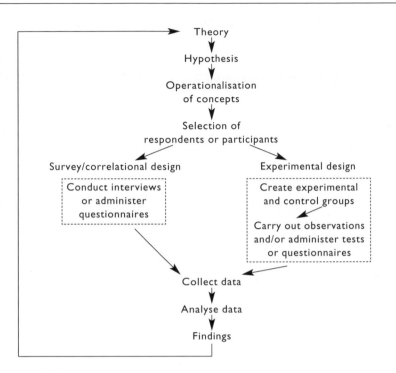

Figure 1.1 The research process

Hypothesis

Once a theory has been formulated, it is likely that researchers will want to test it. Does the theory hold water when faced with empirical evidence? However, it is rarely possible to test a theory as such. Instead, we are more likely to find that a hypothesis, which relates to a limited facet of the theory, will be deduced from the theory and submitted to a searching enquiry. For example, Hirschi, drawing upon his control theory, stipulates that children who are tied to conventional society (in the sense of adhering to conventional values and participating or aspiring to participate in conventional values) will be less likely to commit delinquent acts than those not so tied. Hypotheses very often take the form of relationships between two or more entities – in this case commitment to conventional society and juvenile delinquency. These 'entities' are usually referred to as 'concepts', that is, categories in which are stored our ideas and observations about common elements in the world. The nature of concepts is discussed in greater detail in Chapter 4. Although hypotheses have the advantage that they force researchers to think systematically about what they want to study and to structure their research plans accordingly, they exhibit a potential disadvantage in that they may divert a researcher's attention too far away from other interesting facets of the data he or she has amassed.

Operationalisation of concepts

In order to assess the validity of a hypothesis it is necessary to develop measures of the constituent concepts. This process is often referred to as *operationalisation*, following expositions of the measurement process in physics (Bridgman, 1927). In effect, what is happening here is the translation of the concepts into variables, that is, attributes on which relevant objects (individuals, firms, nations, or whatever) differ. Hirschi operationalised the idea of commitment to conventional society in a number of ways. One route was through a question on a questionnaire asking the children to whom it was to be administered whether they liked school. Delinquency was measured in one of two ways, one of which was to ask about the number of delinquent acts to which children admitted (that is, self-reported delinquent acts). In much experimental research in psychology, the measurement of concepts is achieved through the observation of people, rather than through the administration of questionnaires. For example, if the researcher is interested in aggression, a laboratory situation may be set up in which variations in aggressive behaviour are observed. Another way in which concepts may be operationalised is through the analysis of existing statistics, of which Durkheim's ([1898] 1952) classic analysis of suicide rates is an example. A number of issues to do with the process of devising measures of concepts and some of the properties that measures should possess are discussed in Chapter 4.

Selection of respondents or subjects

If a survey investigation is being undertaken, the researcher must find relevant people to whom the research instrument that has been devised (for example, self-administered questionnaire, interview schedule) should be administered. Hirschi, for example, randomly selected over 5,500 school children from an area in California. The fact of random selection is important here because it reflects a commitment to the production of findings that can be generalised beyond the confines of those who participate in a study. It is rarely possible to contact all units in a population, so a *sample* invariably has to be selected. In order to be able to generalise to a wider population, a *representative sample*, such as one that can be achieved through random sampling, will be required. Moreover, many of the statistical techniques to be covered in this book are *inferential statistics*, which allow the researcher to demonstrate the probability that the results deriving from a sample are likely to be found in the population from which the sample was taken, but only if a random sample has been selected. These issues are examined in Chapter 6.

Setting up a research design

There are two basic types of research design that are employed by psychologists and sociologists. The former tend to use *experimental* designs in which the researcher actively manipulates aspects of a setting, either in the laboratory or in a field situation, and observes the effects of that manipulation on experimental subjects. There must also be a 'control group' which acts as a point of comparison with the group of subjects who receive the experimental manipulation. With a *survey/correlational* design, the researcher does not manipulate any of the variables of interest and data relating to all variables are collected simultaneously. The term *correlation* also refers to a technique for analysing relationships between variables (see Chapter 8), but is used in the present context to denote a type of research design. The researcher does not always have a choice regarding which of the two designs can be adopted. For example, Hirschi could not *make* some children committed to school and others less committed and observe the effects on their propensity to commit delinquent acts. Some variables, like most of those studied by sociologists, are not capable of manipulation. However, there are areas of research in which topics and hypotheses are addressed with both types of research design (for example, the study of the effects of participation at work on job satisfaction and performance – see Bryman, 1986; Locke and Schweiger, 1979). It should be noted that in most cases, therefore, the nature of the research design – whether experimental or survey/correlational – is known at the outset of the sequence signified by Figure 1.1, so that research design characteristics permeate and inform a number of stages of the research process. The nature of the research design has implications for the kinds of statistical manipulation that can be performed on the resulting data. The differences between the two designs are given greater attention in the next section.

Collect data

The researcher collects data at this stage, by interview, questionnaire, observation or whatever. The technicalities of the issues pertinent to this stage are not usually associated with a book such as this. Readers should consult a textbook concerned with social and psychological research methods if they are unfamiliar with the relevant issues.

Analyse data

This stage connects very directly with the material covered in this book. At a minimum, the researcher is likely to want to describe his or her subjects in terms of the variables deriving from the study. For example, the researcher might be interested in the proportion of children who claim to have committed no, just one, or two or more delinquent acts. The various ways of analysing and presenting the information relating to a single variable (sometimes called *univariate analysis*) are examined in Chapter 5. However, the analysis of a single variable is unlikely to suffice and the researcher will probably be interested in the connection between that variable and each of a number of other variables, that is, *bivariate analysis*. The examination of connections among variables can take either of two forms. A researcher who has conducted an experiment may be interested in the extent to which experimental and control groups differ in some respect. For example, the researcher might be interested in examining whether watching violent films increases aggressiveness. The experimental group (which watches the violent films) and the control group (which does not) can then be compared to see how far they differ. The techniques for examining differences are explored in Chapter 7. The researcher may be interested in relationships between variables – are two variables connected with each other so that they tend to vary together? For example, Hirschi (1969: 121) presents a table which shows how liking school and self-reported delinquent acts are interconnected. He found that whereas only 9 per cent of children who say they like school have committed two or more delinquent acts, 49 per cent of those who say they dislike school have committed as many delinquent acts. The ways in which relationships among pairs of variables can be elucidated can be found in Chapter 8. Very often the researcher will be interested in exploring connections among more than two variables, that is, *multivariate analysis*. Chapter 9 examines such analysis in the context of the exploration of differences, while Chapter 10 looks at the multivariate analysis of relationships among more than two variables. The distinction between studying differences and studying relationships is not always clear-cut. We might find that boys are more likely than girls to commit delinquent acts. This finding could be taken to mean that boys and girls differ in terms of propensity to engage in delinquent acts or that there is a relationship between gender and delinquency.

Findings

If the analysis of data suggests that a hypothesis is confirmed, this result can be fed back into the theory that prompted it. Future researchers can then concern themselves either with seeking to replicate the finding or with other ramifications of the theory. However, the refutation of a hypothesis can be just as important in that it may suggest that the theory is faulty or at the very least in need of revision. Sometimes, the hypothesis may be confirmed in some respects only. For example, a multivariate analysis may suggest that a relationship between two variables pertains only to some members of a sample, but not others (for example, women but not men, or younger but not older people). Such a finding will require a reformulation of the theory. Not all findings will necessarily relate directly to a hypothesis. With a social survey, for example, the researcher may collect data on topics whose relevance only becomes evident at a later juncture.

As suggested above, the sequence depicted in Figure 1.1 constitutes a model of the research process, which may not always be reproduced in reality. None the less, it does serve to pinpoint the importance to the process of quantitative research of developing measures of concepts and the thorough analysis of subsequent data. One point that was not mentioned in the discussion is the *form* that the hypotheses and findings tend to assume. One of the main aims of much quantitative research in the social sciences is the demonstration of *causality* – that one variable has an impact upon another. The terms *independent variable* and *dependent variable* are often employed in this context. The former denotes a variable that has an impact upon the dependent variable. The latter, in other words, is deemed to be an effect of the independent variable. This causal imagery is widespread in the social sciences and a major role of multivariate analysis is the elucidation of such causal relationships (Bryman, 1988a). The ease with which a researcher can establish cause and effect relationships is strongly affected by the nature of the research design, and it is to this topic that we shall now turn.

CAUSALITY AND RESEARCH DESIGN

As suggested in the previous paragraph, one of the chief preoccupations among quantitative researchers is to establish causality. This preoccupation in large part derives from a concern to establish findings similar to those of the natural sciences, which often take a causal form. Moreover, findings which establish cause and effect can have considerable practical importance: if we know that one thing affects another, we can manipulate the cause to produce an effect. In much the same way that our knowledge that smoking may cause a number of illnesses, such as lung cancer and heart disease, the social scientist is able to provide potentially practical information by demonstrating causal relationships in appropriate settings.

To say that something causes something else is not to suggest that the dependent variable (the effect) is totally influenced by the independent variable (the cause). You do not necessarily contract a disease if you smoke and many of the diseases contracted by people who smoke may also afflict those who never smoke. 'Cause' here should be taken to mean that variation in the dependent variable is affected by variation in the independent variable. Those who smoke a lot are more likely than those who smoke less, who in turn are more likely than those who do not smoke at all, to contract a variety of diseases that are associated with smoking. Similarly, if we find that watching violence on television induces aggressive behaviour, we are not saying that only people who watch televised violence will behave aggressively, nor that only those people who behave aggressively watch violent television programmes. Causal relationships are invariably about the likelihood of an effect occurring in the light of particular levels of the cause: aggressive behaviour may be more likely to occur when a lot of television violence is watched and people who watch relatively little television violence may be less likely to behave aggressively.

Establishing causality

In order to establish a causal relationship, three criteria have to be fulfilled. First, it is necessary to establish that there is an apparent relationship between two variables. This means that it is necessary to demonstrate that the distribution of values of one variable corresponds to the distribution of values of another variable. Table

1.1 provides information for ten children on the number of aggressive acts they exhibit when they play in two groups of five for two hours per group. The point to note is that there is a relationship between the two variables in that the distribution of values for number of aggressive acts coincides with the distribution for the amount of televised violence watched – children who watch more violence exhibit more aggression than those who watch little violence. The relationship is not perfect: three pairs of children – 3 and 4, 6 and 7 and 9 and 10 – record the same number of aggressive acts, even though they watch different amounts of television violence. Moreover, 8 exhibits more aggression than 6 or 7, even though the latter watch more violence. None the less, a clear pattern is evident which suggests that there is a relationship between the two variables.

Second, it is necessary to demonstrate that the relationship is *non-spurious*. A spurious relationship occurs when there is not a 'true' relationship between two variables that appear to be connected. The variation exhibited by each variable is affected by a common variable. Imagine that the first five children are boys and the second five are girls. This would suggest that gender has a considerable impact on both variables. Boys are more likely than girls both to watch more television violence *and* to exhibit greater aggressiveness. There is still a slight tendency for watching more violence and aggression to be related for both boys and girls, but these tendencies are far less pronounced than for the ten children as a whole. In other words, gender affects each of the two variables. It is because boys are much more likely than girls both to watch more television violence and to behave aggressively that Figure 1.2 illustrates the nature of such a spurious relationship.

Third, it is necessary to establish that the cause precedes the effect, that is, the *time order* of the two related variables. In other words, we must establish that aggression is a consequence of watching televised violence and not the other way around. An effect simply cannot come before a cause. This may seem an extremely obvious criterion that is easy to demonstrate, but, as we shall see, it constitutes a very considerable problem for non-experimental research designs.

Table 1.1 Data on television violence and aggression

Child	Number of hours of violence watched on television per week	Number of aggressive acts recorded
1	9.50	9
2	9.25	8
3	8.75	7
4	8.25	7
5	8.00	6
6	5.50	4
7	5.25	4
8	4.75	5
9	4.50	3
10	4.00	3

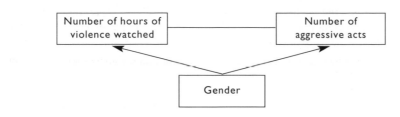

Figure 1.2 A spurious relationship

Causality and experimental designs

A research design provides the basic structure within which an investigation takes place. While a number of different designs can be found, a basic distinction is that between experimental and non-experimental research designs, of which the survey/correlational is the most prominent. In an experiment, the elucidation of cause and effect is an explicit feature of the framework. The term *internal validity* is often employed as an attribute of research and indicates whether the causal findings deriving from an investigation are relatively unequivocal. An internally valid study is one which provides firm evidence of cause and effect. Experimental designs are especially strong in respect of internal validity; this attribute is scarcely surprising in view of the fact that they have been developed specifically in order to generate findings which indicate cause and effect.

Imagine that we wanted to establish that watching violence on television enhances aggression in children. We might conceive of the following study: we bring together a group of ten children; they are allowed to interact and play for two hours, during which the number of aggressive acts committed by each child is recorded by observers, and the children are then exposed to a television programme with a great deal of violence. Such exposure is often called the experimental treatment. They are then allowed a further two-hour period of play and interaction. Aggressive behaviour is recorded in exactly the same way. What we have here is a sequence which runs

$$Obs_1 \; Exp \; Obs_2$$

where Obs_1 is the initial measurement of aggressive behaviour (often called the *pre-test*), Exp is the experimental treatment which allows the independent variable to be introduced, and Obs_2 is the subsequent measurement of aggression (often called the *post-test*).

Let us say that Obs_2 is 30 per cent higher than Obs_1, suggesting that aggressive behaviour has increased substantially. Does this mean that we can say that the increase in aggression was caused by the violence? We cannot make such an attribution because there are alternative explanations of the presumed causal connection. The children may well have become more aggressive over time simply as a consequence of being together and becoming irritated by each other. The researchers may not have given the children enough food or drink and this may have contributed to their bad humour. There is even the possibility that different observers were used for the pre- and post-tests who used different criteria of aggressiveness. So long as we cannot discount these alternative explanations, a definitive conclusion about causation cannot be proffered.

Anyone familiar with the natural sciences will know that an important facet of a properly conducted experiment is that it is controlled so that potentially contaminating factors are minimised. In order to control the contaminating factors that have been mentioned (and therefore to allow the alternative explanations to be rejected), a *control group* is required. This group has exactly the same cluster of experiences as the group which receives the first treatment – known as the *experimental group* – but it does not receive the experimental treatment. In the context of our imaginary television study, we now have two groups of children who are exposed to exactly the same conditions, except that one group watches the violent films (the experimental group) and the second group has no experimental treatment (the control group). This design is illustrated in Figure 1.3. The two groups' experiences have to be as similar as possible, so that only the experimental group's exposure to the experimental treatment distinguishes them.

It is also necessary to ensure that the members of the two groups are as similar as possible. This is achieved by taking a sample of children and *randomly assigning* them to either the experimental or the control group. If random assignment is not carried out, there is always the possibility that differences between the two groups can be attributed to divergent personal or other characteristics. For example, there may be more boys than girls in one group, or differences in the ethnic composition of the two groups. Such differences in personal or background characteristics would mean that the ensuing findings could not be validly attributed to the independent variable, and to that factor alone.

Let us say that the difference between Obs_1 and Obs_2 is 30 per cent and between Obs_3 and Obs_4 is 28 per cent. If this were the case, we would conclude that the difference between the two groups is so small that it appears that the experimental treatment (Exp) has made no difference to the increase in aggression; in other words, aggression in the experimental group would probably have increased anyway. The frustration of being together too long or insufficient food or drink or some other factor probably accounts for the Obs_2–Obs_1 difference. However, if the difference between Obs_3 and Obs_4 was only 3 per cent, we would be much more prepared to say that watching violence has increased aggression in the experi-

	Obs_1	Exp	Obs_2	*Experimental group*
Random	(Aggression level)	(Watch violence)	(Aggression level)	
assignment				
	Obs_3	Exp	Obs_4	*Control group*
	(Aggression level)	(Do not watch violence)	(Aggression level)	

Figure 1.3 An experiment

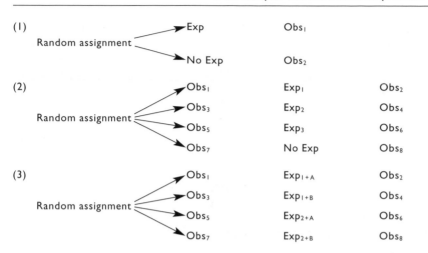

Figure 1.4 Three types of experimental design

mental group. It would suggest that around 27 per cent of the increase in aggressive behaviour in the experimental group (that is, $30-3$) can be attributed to the experimental treatment. Differences between experimental and control groups are not usually as clear-cut as in this illustration, since often the difference between the groups is fairly small. Statistical tests are necessary in this context to determine the probability of obtaining such a difference by chance. Such tests are described in Chapters 7 and 9.

In this imaginary investigation, the three criteria of causality are met, and therefore if we did find that the increase in the dependent variable was considerably greater for the experimental group than the control group we could have considerable confidence in saying that watching television violence caused greater aggression. First, a relationship is established by demonstrating that subjects watching television violence exhibited greater aggression than those who did not. Second, the combination of a control group and random assignment allows the possibility of the relationship being spurious to be eliminated, since other factors which may impinge on the two variables would apply equally to the two groups. Third, the time order of the variables is demonstrated by the increase in aggressive behaviour succeeding the experimental group's exposure to the television violence. Precisely because the independent variable is manipulated by the researcher, time order can be easily demonstrated, since the effects of the manipulation can be directly gauged. Thus, we could say confidently that Watching television violence → Aggressive behaviour since the investigation exhibits a high degree of internal validity.

There is a variety of different types of experimental design. These are briefly summarised in Figure 1.4. In the first design, there is no pre-test, just a comparison between the experimental and control groups in terms of the dependent variable. With the second design, there are a number of groups. This is a frequent occurrence in the social sciences, where one is more likely to be interested in different levels or types of the independent variable rather than simply its presence or absence. Thus, in the television violence context, we could envisage four groups consisting of different degrees of violence. The third design, a *factorial* design, occurs where the researcher is interested in the effects of more than one independent variable on the dependent variable. The researcher might be interested in whether the presence of adults in close proximity reduces children's propensity to behave aggressively. We might then have four possible combinations deriving from the manipulation of each of the two independent variables. For example, Exp_{1+A} would mean a combination of watching violence and adults in close proximity; Exp_{1+B} would be watching violence and no adults in close proximity.

SURVEY DESIGN AND CAUSALITY

When a social survey is carried out, the nature of the research design is very different from the experiment. The survey usually entails the collection of data on a number of variables at a single juncture. The researcher might be interested in the relationship between people's political attitudes and behaviour on the one hand, and a number of other variables such as each respondent's occupation, social background, race, gender, age, and various non-political attitudes. But none of these variables is manipulated as in the experiment. Indeed, many variables cannot be manipulated and their relationships with other variables can only be examined through a social survey. We cannot make some people old, others young, and still others middle-aged and then observe the effects of age on political attitudes. Moreover, not only are variables not manipulated in a social survey study, data on variables are simultaneously collected so that it is not possible to establish a time order of the variables in question. In an experiment, a time order can be discerned in that the effect of the manipulated independent variable on the dependent variable is directly observed. These characteristics are not solely associated with research using interviews or questionnaires. Many studies using archival statistics, such as those collected by governments and organisations, exhibit the same characteristics, since data are often available in relation to a number of variables for a particular year.

Survey designs are often called *correlational* designs to denote the tendency for such research to be able to reveal relationships between variables and to draw attention to their limited capacity in connection with the elucidation of causal processes. Precisely because in survey research variables are not manipulated (and often are not capable of manipulation), the ability of the researcher to impute cause and effect is limited. Let us say that we collect data on manual workers' levels of job satisfaction and productivity in a firm. We may find, through the kinds of techniques examined in Chapter 8 of this book, that there is a strong relationship between the two, suggesting that workers who exhibit high levels of job satisfaction also have high levels of productivity. We can say that there is a relationship

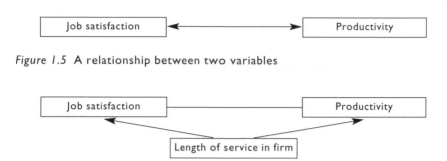

Figure 1.5 A relationship between two variables

Figure 1.6 Is the relationship spurious?

between the two variables (see Figure 1.5), but as we have seen, this is only a first step in the demonstration of causality. It is also necessary to confirm that the relationship is non-spurious. For example, could it be that workers who have been with the firm a long time are both more satisfied and more productive (see Figure 1.6)? The ways in which the possibility of non-spuriousness can be checked are examined in Chapter 10.

However, the third hurdle – establishing that the putative cause precedes the putative effect – is extremely difficult. The problem is that either of the two possibilities depicted in Figure 1.7 may be true. Job satisfaction may cause greater productivity, but it has long been recognised that the causal connection may work the other way around (that is, if you are good at your job you often enjoy it more). Because data relating to each of the two variables have been simultaneously collected, it is not possible to arbitrate between the two versions of causality presented in Figure 1.7. One way of dealing with this problem is through a reconstruction of the likely causal order of the variables involved. Sometimes this process of inference can be fairly uncontroversial. For example, if we find a relationship between race and number of years spent in formal schooling, we can say that the former affects the latter. However, this modelling of likely causal connections is more fraught when it is not obvious which variable precedes the other, as with the relationship between job satisfaction and productivity. When such difficulties arise, it may be necessary to include a second wave of data collection in relation to the same respondents in order to see, for example, whether the impact of job satisfaction on subsequent productivity is greater than the impact of productivity on subsequent job satisfaction. Such a design is known as a *panel design* (Cramer, 1996), but is not very common in the social sciences. The bulk of

Figure 1.7 Two possible causal interpretations of a relationship

the discussion in this book about non-experimental research will be concerned with the survey/correlational design in which data on variables are simultaneously collected.

The procedures involved in making causal inferences from survey data are examined in Chapter 10 in the context of the multivariate analysis of relationships among variables. The chief point to be gleaned from the preceding discussion is that the extraction of causal connections among variables can be undertaken with greater facility in the context of experimental research than when survey data are being analysed.

EXERCISES

1   What is the chief difference between univariate, bivariate and multivariate quantitative data analysis?
2   Why is random assignment crucial to a true experimental design?
3   A researcher collects data by interview on a sample of households to find out if people who read 'quality' daily newspapers are more knowledgeable about politics than people who read 'tabloid' newspapers daily. The hunch was confirmed. People who read the quality newspapers were twice as likely to respond accurately to a series of questions designed to test their political knowledge. The researcher concludes that the quality dailies induce higher levels of political knowledge than the tabloids. Assess this reasoning.

Chapter 2

Analysing data with computers

First steps with SPSS 10 for Windows

Since the different kinds of statistics to be described in this book will be carried out with one of the, if not the, most widely used and comprehensive statistical programs in the social sciences, SPSS, we will begin by outlining what this entails. The abbreviation SPSS stands for *Statistical Package for the Social Sciences*. This package of programs is available for both personal and mainframe (or multi-user) computers. These programs are being continuously updated and so there are various versions in existence.

Currently there are two main kinds of *operating system* for computers. The traditional system, still employed by mainframe (or multi-user) computers, requires *commands* and names to be typed in. The more recent system uses *menus* and *dialog boxes* from which these commands and names can be selected by *keys* or a *mouse*, although commands can also be typed in. This latter system was originally developed for Macintosh personal computers and is now available for a Windows environment on IBM-compatible personal computers with a 386 or higher processor. The version for Windows 3.1 is known as SPSS Release 6, which we have outlined in an earlier book (Bryman and Cramer, 1997). After the introduction of Windows 95, a new release of SPSS (Release 7) was designed to run on this operating system. The latest version for Windows 95/98 is Release 10. This book describes the use of Release 10, which we shall refer to as SPSS for short unless otherwise indicated. The use of Releases 8 and 9 was described in the previous edition of this book (Bryman and Cramer, 1999).

The great advantage of using a package like SPSS is that it enables you to score and to analyse quantitative data very quickly and in many different ways once you have learned how. In other words, it will help you to eliminate those long hours spent working out scores, carrying out involved calculations, and making those inevitable mistakes that so frequently occur while doing this. It will also provide you with the opportunity to use more complicated and often more appropriate statistical techniques which you would not have dreamed of attempting otherwise.

There is, of course, what may seem to be a strong initial disadvantage in using computer programs to analyse data, which is that you will have to learn how to run these programs. The time spent doing this, however, will be much less than doing these same calculations by hand. In addition, you will have picked up some knowledge which should be of value to you in a world where the use of computers is fast becoming increasingly common. The ability to do things quickly and with little effort is also much more fun and often easier than you might at first imagine.

When mastering a new skill, like SPSS, it is inevitable that you will make mistakes which can be frustrating and off-putting. While this is something we all do, it may seem that we make many more mistakes when learning to use a computer than we do carrying out other activities. The reason for this is that programs require instructions to be given in a very precise form and usually in a particular sequence in order for them to work. This precision may be less obvious or true of other everyday things that we do. It is worth remembering, however, that these errors will not harm the computer or its program in any way.

In order to make as few mistakes as possible, it is important at this stage to follow precisely the instructions laid down for the examples in this and subsequent chapters. Although 'bugs' do sometimes occur, errors are usually the result of something you have done and not the fault of the machine or the program. The program will tell you what the error is if there is something wrong with the form of the instructions you have given it, but not if you have told it to add up the wrong set of numbers. In other words, it questions the presentation but not the objectives of the instructions.

THE DATA FILE

Before you can analyse data, you need to create a file which holds them. To illustrate the way in which these files are produced, we shall use an imaginary set of data from a questionnaire study which is referred to as the Job Survey. The data relating to this study derive from two sources: a questionnaire study of employees who answer questions about themselves and a questionnaire study of their supervisors who answer questions relating to each of the employees. The questions asked are shown in Appendix 2.1 at the end of this chapter, while the coding of the information or data collected is presented in Table 2.1. The cases consist of people, traditionally called *respondents* by sociologists and *subjects* by psychologists whose preferred term now is *participants*. Although questionnaire data have been used as an example, it should be recognised that SPSS and the data analysis procedures described in this book may be used with other forms of quantitative data, such as official statistics or observational measures.

As the data set is relatively large, it may be more convenient to let skilled personnel enter the data into a file for you if you have access to such a service. If you do, they may enter it into what is called a simple text or ASCII file. ASCII stands for American Standard Code for Information Interchange and is widely used for transferring information from one computer to another. You then read this data file into SPSS. If you do not have access to such a service or if the data set is small, then it may be easier for you to enter the data directly into an SPSS window called **Data Editor**. Both these procedures are described later in this chapter.

Table 2.1 The Job Survey data

01	1	1	16600	29	1	4	0	3	4	4	2	4	2	2	2	2	3	2	2	3	0	1	7
02	2	1	14600	26	5	2	0	0	2	3	2	2	1	2	3	4	4	4	1	3	4	4	8
03	3	1	17800	40	5	4	4	4	4	1	2	1	2	2	2	1	2	3	1	4	3	4	0
04	3	1	16400	46	15	2	2	5	2	4	1	2	2	2	3	2	2	3	2	3	3	4	4
05	2	2	18600	63	36	4	3	4	4	1	2	3	3	3	4	5	5	4	1	3	5	3	0
06	1	1	16000	54	31	2	2	5	3	3	2	1	1	2	4	4	4	4	1	1	3	4	1
07	1	1	16600	29	2	0	3	3	2	3	2	2	3	2	3	5	4	2	2	3	5	2	0
08	3	1	17600	35	2	5	2	2	4	2	3	4	3	2	3	3	3	2	2	3	4	4	2
09	2	2	17600	33	4	3	3	1	2	4	2	3	4	1	2	2	3	2	2	2	1	1	5
10	2	2	13800	27	6	4	3	2	3	3	2	1	3	2	3	4	3	5	1	2	2	4	4
11	1	1	14200	29	4	2	2	4	1	4	2	1	1	2	5	4	3	4	2	2	2	3	8
12	2	1	0	19	2	1	1	5	2	4	1	1	1	1	3	4	3	3	1	3	2	3	4
13	4	1	18000	55	35	3	3	3	4	2	2	2	3	2	5	5	5	4	1	4	3	5	1
14	1	2	17000	29	1	2	3	4	2	4	2	2	3	1	4	3	4	4	1	1	2	2	0
15	3	1	18200	48	8	3	3	2	2	1	3	2	4	4	2	3	3	3	2	4	5	5	1
16	2	1	15800	32	7	3	3	4	2	2	2	3	1	2	4	2	2	2	2	2	2	3	4
17	1	1	16600	48	14	3	3	3	2	4	1	2	2	2	4	5	4	4	1	2	5	3	1
18	1	2	13400	18	1	2	2	4	2	4	2	3	2	2	5	5	5	1	1	2	3	3	6
19	3	2	15000	28	2	4	4	2	3	2	3	4	3	3	3	2	3	2	2	3	4	4	3
20	3	2	17600	37	1	3	2	3	3	3	3	2	1	2	5	4	4	5	1	1	4	1	3
21	1	1	0	43	16	1	4	4	3	3	3	2	3	3	3	2	4	4	2	4	5	2	6
22	1	1	17400	39	6	3	2	3	2	3	3	2	2	3	4	3	5	3	2	1	1	5	5
23	1	1	18000	53	5	1	4	3	4	4	4	3	2	2	3	5	4	2	1	3	3	5	13
24	2	2	16000	34	9	1	3	4	1	5	1	2	1	1	3	4	4	3	2	1	3	3	9
25	3	2	17000	43	17	4	3	4	5	3	3	1	3	2	3	2	4	4	1	3	5	2	2
26	1	1	14000	21	1	4	4	2	2	3	4	3	3	4	2	3	2	2	1	2	5	5	3
27	1	1	16200	50	28	3	2	3	3	4	2	1	1	2	5	5	5	4	1	2	2	4	8
28	1	2	12400	31	9	1	2	5	1	4	2	2	1	2	4	4	5	4	2	3	5	5	0
29	1	1	13600	31	12	3	3	4	3	3	3	2	2	3	2	3	1	2	1	3	5	4	6
30	2	2	16400	52	21	2	3	2	3	2	3	3	3	3	2	2	2	2	2	4	4	3	10
31	1	1	14400	54	12	3	5	3	3	3	3	2	3	2	4	3	4	4	2	4	4	2	99
32	3	2	12400	28	10	2	2	4	1	5	1	2	2	2	3	3	3	2	1	2	4	4	9
33	2	2	16600	50	23	4	4	3	4	3	4	2	3	4	3	3	3	3	2	3	4	5	5
34	2	2	16000	52	21	5	4	3	3	3	3	4	3	3	2	3	3	2	1	3	2	5	4
35	1	2	15000	40	21	1	1	3	4	3	3	2	2	3	2	2	2	1	2	2	3	6	
36	2	1	11800	19	1	2	2	5	2	4	2	1	2	2	5	5	5	5	2	2	3	2	3
37	2	1	17600	38	4	5	4	1	4	3	5	3	3	3	2	1	2	1	2	4	4	4	8
38	2	1	18000	61	41	5	3	2	4	1	3	2	2	2	2	2	1	2	2	3	5	4	3
39	1	2	15600	37	8	3	2	4	2	3	2	3	3	2	4	5	4	5	1	3	4	4	8
40	2	1	13400	31	5	2	2	5	2	5	2	2	2	1	5	5	5	4	2	1	1	2	5
41	2	2	15000	43	21	4	3	2	2	2	3	4	2	3	3	3	3	3	1	1	4	2	0
42	3	1	13600	23	3	1	2	5	3	5	1	1	2	1	4	4	4	5	1	3	2	2	8
43	2	2	14000	27	5	1	1	4	1	4	1	1	1	2	4	5	4	4	2	1	2	1	9
44	1	1	15000	28	7	3	3	1	3	3	3	5	3	3	1	2	2	1	1	2	4	3	9
45	1	1	13200	0	10	1	1	4	1	4	2	2	2	2	4	2	5	5	1	4	1	3	10
46	3	1	13400	18	1	4	2	3	4	2	2	3	3	2	4	3	5	4	1	4	3	4	3
47	1	2	20600	48	23	3	4	3	3	3	2	2	3	2	2	1	3	2	2	4	4	3	8
48	1	2	13600	29	10	2	3	5	4	4	2	2	2	1	3	4	2	2	1	3	4	4	11
49	1	2	14600	42	10	2	2	3	3	3	2	2	1	2	5	5	5	5	2	1	4	4	0
50	1	1	18200	53	12	4	5	2	5	1	4	5	3	4	2	2	2	2	2	4	4	4	1

continued

Table 2.1 continued

51	1	1	15200	32	12	3	2	4	1	4	3	2	2	3	3	3	4	2	1	2	3	2	1
52	1	2	13000	31	2	1	3	5	1	5	2	2	3	2	5	4	4	5	2	1	3	1	8
53	1	1	19000	55	19	5	4	3	5	3	5	4	3	3	3	4	3	3	1	3	4	3	0
54	3	2	14800	26	8	4	4	1	3	3	4	5	2	3	1	2	1	2	2	4	3	3	2
55	1	2	17200	53	22	3	4	2	3	1	3	4	4	3	2	1	2	2	1	3	5	5	0
56	1	1	15600	51	31	2	3	3	3	3	3	2	4	4	5	4	5	5	1	4	1	1	8
57	1	1	15400	48	23	3	1	4	3	4	2	2	2	2	5	5	4	5	1	1	3	2	6
58	1	2	13800	48	28	1	1	4	1	5	2	2	2	1	5	5	5	5	2	1	4	3	4
59	2	2	15800	62	40	1	2	3	2	5	2	2	3	2	5	4	4	5	2	1	1	5	7
60	2	1	17400	57	13	2	3	4	2	3	2	3	1	2	3	3	4	3	1	4	4	1	4
61	1	2	17800	42	20	5	4	2	2	2	3	3	3	3	2	1	2	4	2	3	3	3	2
62	1	1	14200	21	2	1	2	3	1	4	2	3	2	1	3	3	3	3	1	4	2	2	0
63	3	2	12800	26	8	3	1	3	2	4	1	2	1	1	2	3	3	2	1	4	1	1	4
64	1	2	13600	46	0	1	2	5	2	4	3	1	2	2	5	5	5	5	2	2	3	4	5
65	1	2	21000	59	21	4	3	2	4	2	2	2	3	3	2	3	2	2	2	4	5	1	4
66	4	2	14200	30	8	0	3	3	2	4	2	3	2	2	5	4	4	4	1	2	2	3	2
67	1	1	14600	29	8	3	2	2	3	3	2	3	2	1	5	3	4	3	2	1	4	5	10
68	3	1	13800	45	9	2	3	4	3	4	3	3	3	3	3	4	3	3	2	2	3	4	9
69	3	1	16000	53	30	3	2	5	3	2	2	1	2	2	4	5	3	4	2	2	1	4	2
70	1	1	13800	47	22	2	3	4	2	5	2	3	4	2	4	3	5	4	1	2	4	4	11

With a simple text file, the data are put into a space which consists of a large number of rows, comprising a maximum of eighty columns in many computers. Each column in a row can only take one character such as a single digit. The data for the same variable are always placed in the same column(s) in a row and a row always contains the data of the same object of analysis or **case**. Cases are often people, but can be any unit of interest such as families, schools, hospitals, regions or nations.

Since it is easier to analyse data consisting of numbers rather than a mixture of numbers and other characters such as alphabetic letters, all of the variables or answers in the Job Survey have been coded as numbers. So, for instance, each of the five possible answers to the first question has been given a number varying from 1 to 5. If the respondent has put a tick against White/European, then this response is coded as 1. (Although the use of these categories may be questioned, as may many of the concepts in the social sciences, this kind of information is sometimes collected in surveys and is used here as an example of a categorical (nominal) variable. We shall shorten the name of the first category to 'white' throughout the book to simplify matters.) It is preferable in designing question-naires that, wherever possible, numbers should be clearly assigned to particular answers so that little else needs to be done to the data before they are typed in by someone else. Before multiple copies of the questionnaire are made, it is always worth checking with the person who types in this information that this has been adequately done.

It is also important to reserve a number for *missing data*, such as a failure to give a clear and unambiguous response, since we need to record this information. Numbers which represent real or non-missing data should not be used to code missing values. Thus, for example, since the answers to the first question on ethnic group in the Job Survey are coded 1 to 5, it is necessary to use some other number to identify a missing response. In this survey all missing data except that for absenteeism have been coded as zero since this value cannot be confused with the way that non-missing data are represented. Because some employees have not been absent from work (that is, zero days), missing data for absenteeism could not be coded as '0'. Instead, it is indicated by '99' since no employee has been away that long. Sometimes it might be necessary to distinguish different kinds of missing data, such as a 'Don't know' response from a 'Does not apply' one, in which case these two answers would be represented by different numbers.

It is advisable to give each participant an identifying number to be able to refer to them if necessary. This number should be placed in the first few columns of each row or line. Since there are seventy participants, only columns 1 and 2 need to be used for this purpose. If there were 100 participants, then the first three columns would be required to record this information as the largest number consists of three digits. One empty or blank space will be left between columns containing data for different variables to make the file easier to read, although it is not necessary to do this.

Since all the data for one participant can be fitted on to one line using this fixed format, only one line needs to be reserved for each participant in this instance, and the data for the next participant can be put into the second line. If more than one line were required to record all the data for one participant, then you would use as many subsequent rows as were needed to do so. In this case, it may also be worth giving each of the lines of data for a particular participant an identifying number to help you read the information more readily, so that the first line would be coded 1, the second 2, and so on. Each line or row of data for a participant is known as a **record** in SPSS.

The first variable in our survey and our data file refers to the racial or ethnic origin of our respondents. Since this can only take one of six values (if we include the possibility that they might not have answered this question), then these data can be put into one column. If we leave a space between the participant's two-digit identification number and the one-digit number representing their ethnic group, then the data for this latter variable will be placed in column 4. Since the second variable of gender can also be coded as a single digit number, this information is placed in column 6. The third variable of current gross annual income, however, requires five columns of space since all participants earned more than £10,000 but less than £100,000, and so this variable occupies columns 8 to 12 inclusively (please note that the comma and pound sign should not be included when entering the data).

A full listing of the variables and the columns they occupy is presented in Table 2.2. The data file is named **jsr.dat** which is an abbreviation of 'job survey raw data'. Since SPSS accepts letters written in capitals, or upper case (for example, **JSR.DAT**) and small, or lower case (for example, **jsr.dat**), lower-case letters will be used to make typing easier for you. Restrictions and conventions on the form of names will be described later in this chapter.

Table 2.2 The SPSS names and location of the Job Survey variables

Variable name	SPSS name	Column location
Identification number	**id**	1–2
Ethnic group	**ethnicgp**	4
Gender	**gender**	6
Gross annual income	**income**	8–12
Age	**age**	14–15
Years worked	**years**	17–18
Organisational commitment	**commit**	20
Job-satisfaction scale		
Item 1	**satis1**	22
Item 2	**satis2**	24
Item 3	**satis3**	26
Item 4	**satis4**	28
Job-autonomy scale		
Item 1	**autonom1**	30
Item 2	**autonom2**	32
Item 3	**autonom3**	34
Item 4	**autonom4**	36
Job-routine scale		
Item 1	**routine1**	38
Item 2	**routine2**	40
Item 3	**routine3**	42
Item 4	**routine4**	44
Attendance at meeting	**attend**	46
Rated skill	**skill**	48
Rated productivity	**prody**	50
Rated quality	**qual**	52
Absenteeism	**absence**	54–55

GAINING ACCESS TO SPSS

To use SPSS, it is necessary to have access to it via a personal computer. A personal computer consists of a *keyboard* on which you type in your instructions, a *mouse* which provides an alternative way of moving about the screen and selecting instructions, and usually a video display unit (VDU) or television-like *screen* which displays information. While the amount of information shown at any one moment on the screen is necessarily limited, further information can be brought into view with the appropriate use of the keys or the mouse. A personal computer also usually has a printer which can be used to print out information stored in the computer and can be used to print out a record of what you have done. Keyboards are used to type or put in (hence the term *input*) the data that you want to analyse and also the names of variables and files you have created.

The Windows system allows commands to be selected from words or *icons* presented as a menu in a window on the screen. Commands can usually be selected by moving a pointer called a *cursor* on to them with either the keys or, more normally, the mouse, and then pressing the Return key or the left button on the mouse, or in Windows 95/98 by simply selecting the next option. Choosing options with the mouse is generally easier than doing this with keys since it simply involves moving the mouse appropriately. With keys, however, some options are chosen by pressing the relevant cursor keys while others are selected by pressing up to two keys other than the cursor keys. The cursor keys are usually on the right hand side of the keyboard and have arrows on them pointing in the direction in which the cursor is to be moved. You may prefer to use the mouse for some operations and the keys for others.

Start

To access SPSS in the windows environment, select the **Start** button or icon at the bottom of the screen which presents the first column or menu on the left in Box 2.1.

Select **Programs** on this menu which displays the second menu (columns 2 and 3) in Box 2.1. Note that on many computers fewer programs will be listed than shown here.

Select **SPSS for Windows** from this menu, which opens the third menu (at the bottom of column 3) in Box 2.1.

Select **SPSS 10.0 for Windows** which produces the **Data Editor** window in Box 2.2. You can prevent the **SPSS for Windows** dialog box superimposed on the

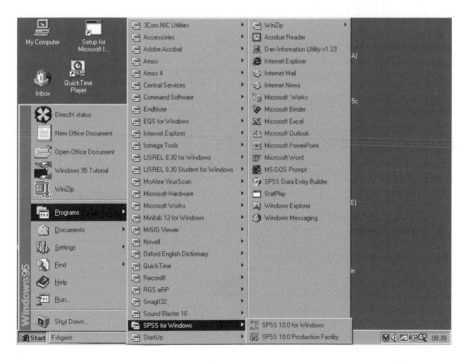

Box 2.1 Windows 95/98 opening window

Box 2.2 SPSS Data Editor

Data Editor being shown on your own computer the next time you access SPSS if you select the **Don't show this dialog in the future** check box near the bottom of the dialog box. Select **Cancel** to remove the dialog to enter data into the cells of the **Data Editor**.

Listed at the top of this window are the names of various procedures such as

Box 2.3 **Data** option drop-down menu

File, **Edit** and so on. To see what these procedures are, we simply move the cursor to a particular option and press the left button on the mouse once. A *drop-down* menu will then appear, as shown in Box 2.3 where the **Data** option has been chosen. To see the other options, simply move the cursor to that option.

The ellipsis, or three dots, after an option term (**...**) on a drop-down menu, such as on the **Select Cases...** option, signifies a dialog box will appear when this option is chosen. If we select this option, for example, the **Select Cases** dialog box displayed in Box 2.4 will appear when data have already been entered into the **Data Editor**. To cancel a dialog box, select the **Cancel** button in the dialog box. A right-facing arrowhead ▶ after an option term such as on the **Merge Files** option, on the other hand, indicates that a further submenu will appear to the right of the drop-down as shown in Box 2.8. An option with neither of these signs means that there are no further drop-down menus to select.

Below these options is a *toolbar* with *buttons* on it. These buttons enable you to carry out procedures directly without having to go to the options and select the appropriate procedure. The functions that the buttons carry out are displayed in a small yellow box near them and in the bottom line of the window. So, for example, the first button says **Open File**. You can add further buttons to the toolbar. The **Help** system described on pp. 33–4 gives instructions on how to do this.

Box 2.4 **Select Cases** dialog box

ENTERING AND EDITING DATA IN DATA EDITOR

The easiest way to enter data in SPSS yourself is to type it directly into the matrix of columns and numbered rows in the **Data Editor** window shown in Box 2.2. Note that in this case a column can hold more than one digit. Initially the cursor will be in the *cell* in the first row of the first column. The *frame* of this cell will be shown in bold to denote that it is the *active* cell. To enter a value in any one cell, make that cell active by moving to it with either the cursor keys or the mouse, type in the value and then move to the next cell into which you want to put a value. Columns are consecutively numbered once you enter a value. So if you enter a value in the fifth column the first five columns will be labelled **var00001** to **var00005**. To change any value already entered, move to the cell containing that value, type in the new value and move to another cell. If you want to leave a cell empty delete the entry with the Backspace or Delete key and move to another cell, when a full stop (.) will be left denoting a missing value.

NAMING VARIABLES IN DATA EDITOR

To name a variable in **Data Editor**, select **Variable View** near the bottom of the window. Select the appropriate row under the **Name** column and type in the name (for example, **ethnicgp** in the first row as shown in Box 2.5).

SPSS NAMES

Variable and file names in SPSS have to meet certain specifications. They must be no longer than eight characters and must begin with an alphabetic character (A–Z). The remaining characters can be any letter, number, period, @ (at), $ (dollar) or _ (underscore). Blank spaces are not allowed and they cannot end with a period and, preferably, not with an underscore. In addition certain words, known as *keywords*, cannot be used because they can only be interpreted as commands by SPSS. They include words such as **add, and, any, or** and **to**, to give but a few examples. If you accidentally use a prohibited keyword as a name, you will be told this is invalid when you try to run this procedure by selecting the **OK** button. No keyword contains numbers so you can be certain that names which include numbers will always be recognised as such. It is important to remember that the same name cannot be used for different variables or files. Thus, for example, you could not use the name **satis** to refer to all four of the questions which measure job satisfaction. You would need to distinguish them in some way, such as calling the answer to the first question **satis1,** the answer to the second one **satis2,** and so on. The SPSS names given to the variables in the Job Survey are presented in Table 2.2.

	Name	Type	Width	Decimals	Label	Values	Missing	Columns	Align	Measure
1	ethnicgp	Numeric	1	0		None	0	8	Right	Ordinal
2	gender	Numeric	1	0		None	None	8	Right	Ordinal
3	income	Numeric	5	0		None	None	8	Right	Scale
4	age	Numeric	2	0		None	None	8	Right	Scale
5	years	Numeric	2	0		None	None	8	Right	Scale
6	commit	Numeric	1	0		None	None	8	Right	Ordinal
7	satis1	Numeric	1	0		None	0	8	Right	Ordinal
8	satis2	Numeric	1	0		None	0	8	Right	Ordinal
9	satis3	Numeric	1	0		None	None	8	Right	Ordinal
10	satis4	Numeric	1	0		None	None	8	Right	Ordinal
11	autonom1	Numeric	1	0		None	None	8	Right	Ordinal
12	autonom2	Numeric	1	0		None	None	8	Right	Ordinal
13	autonom3	Numeric	1	0		None	None	8	Right	Ordinal
14	autonom4	Numeric	1	0		None	None	8	Right	Ordinal
15	routine1	Numeric	1	0		None	None	8	Right	Ordinal
16	routine2	Numeric	1	0		None	None	8	Right	Ordinal
17	routine3	Numeric	1	0		None	None	8	Right	Ordinal
18	routine4	Numeric	1	0		None	None	8	Right	Ordinal
19	attend	Numeric	1	0		None	None	8	Right	Ordinal
20	skill	Numeric	1	0		None	None	8	Right	Ordinal
21	prody	Numeric	1	0		None	None	8	Right	Ordinal
22	qual	Numeric	1	0		None	None	8	Right	Ordinal
23	absence	Numeric	2	0		None	99	8	Right	Ordinal

Box 2.5 **Variable View** window of **Data Editor**

DEFINING OTHER ASPECTS OF VARIABLES IN DATA EDITOR

We can define nine other aspects of variables when naming them. These aspects are listed just above the data matrix and range from **Type** on the left to **Measure** on the right. You may not see all these nine aspects at once. You can change the width of each column by selecting the line next to the name of the column whose width you want to change and moving the column line to the desired position, as we have done in Box 2.5.

The pre-selected settings for these aspects are shown and are known as the default options. If we wish to change any of these settings, we select the appropriate row and column to make the desired change. In general and for our purposes the most important of these other aspects is **Missing** values.

DEFINING MISSING VALUES

In the Job Survey, we have missing values for **income** (cases 12 and 21), **age** (case 45), **satis1** (cases 1 and 2), **satis2** (case 2), **prody** (case 1) and **absence** (case 31). So we have to specify the appropriate missing values for these variables, which are

0 for the first five (**income**, **age**, **satis1**, **satis2** and **prody**) and **99** for the sixth variable called **absence**. We do this by selecting the appropriate row of the **Missing** column in the **Variable View** of the **Data Editor** and then selecting the ellipsis or three dots in that cell. This opens the **Missing Values** dialog box shown in Box 2.6. In our case we select **Discrete missing values**, type the appropriate value in the first box and then select **OK**. If we type in **0**, then **None** in that row of the **Missing** column of **Variable View** will be replaced with **0** as shown in Box 2.5.

If someone else is entering the data, we need to let them know how missing data for any of the variables are to be coded. We could enter this code here to remind us what it is. Thus, in this example, missing data for all variables other than **absence** has been defined as **0**.

DEFINING DECIMAL PLACES

The default number of decimal places is two. For most purposes it is easier to code all variables as numbers, which we have done for the Job Survey. Since all our values are whole numbers we could change **2** to **0** in the **Decimals** column of the **Variable View** window. To do this, we select each row in turn in this column, and select the downwards button to give **0**.

DEFINING VARIABLE AND VALUE LABELS

SPSS variable names are restricted to eight characters, which usually means that they have to be abbreviated, making their meaning less clear. Using this option, variable labels can be created which will be displayed on the output. These variable labels can be very long, although most output will not present very long labels. For example, the SPSS variable name **ethnicgp** could be labelled **ethnic**

Box 2.6 **Missing values** dialog box

group. To do this, we type in this name for the first row of the **Labels** column in the **Variable View** window. If we do this, then the extended variable name will be presented first in the section of dialog boxes where the variable names are listed (for example, Box 2.12) followed by the abbreviated name in brackets. We have used abbreviated names as these are used in the other sections of the dialog boxes and are generally less cumbersome.

We could also label the values of a variable by selecting the appropriate row in the **Values** column (for example, **ethnicgp**) and then selecting the ellipsis, or three dots, in that cell. This opens the **Value Labels** dialog box shown in Box 2.7. Type in the value (for example, **1**) in the box entitled **Value:**, the label (for example, **white**) in the box entitled **Value Label:** and select **Add**. The value labels for the five ethnic groups in the Job Survey are presented in Box 2.7. Value labels can be up to sixty characters long, although most output will not show labels this long. To remove a label we first select it and then **Remove**. To change a label, we first select it, make the desired changes and then select **Change**. When we have what we want, we select **OK** to close the **Value Labels** dialog box.

DEFINING COLUMN FORMAT AND ALIGNMENT

It is unlikely that you would wish to change the width of the column in **Data Editor**, but if you do, select the appropriate row in the **Columns** column and then select the upwards or downwards button to enter your desired value. If you wish to alter the alignment of data within a column, select the appropriate row in the **Align** column, select the downwards arrow and then select one of the other two options.

Defining consecutive variables simultaneously

If you want to define consecutive variables simultaneously with the same format (such as **sat1** to **routine4**), define the first variable (**satis1**), copy that row,

Box 2.7 **Value Labels** dialog box

highlight the subsequent rows to be defined (**9** to **19**), select **Paste** or **Paste Variables...** and re-name variables as appropriate.

SAVING DATA IN DATA EDITOR

When we want to leave SPSS or to work on another data set in the same session, these data and any changes we have made to them will be lost unless we save them as a file. We could save this file on to the hard disk of the computer. However, if others use the computer, they may delete our files. Even if no one else is likely to use the computer, it is necessary to make a *back-up* copy of our files on one or more formatted *floppy disks* in case we should lose them. The floppy disk is inserted into a slot called a *drive*.

To be able to retrieve a file, we need to give it a name. This name can consist of a prefix or *stem* of up to eight characters followed by a full stop and a suffix or *extension* of three characters. The stem name usually refers to the content of the file (such as **jsr** in the case of our **J**ob **S**urvey **r**aw data file) while the extension

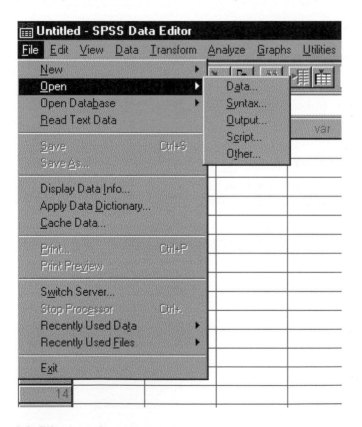

Box 2.8 **File** drop-down menu

Save Data As

Save in: 3½ Floppy (A:)

File name: a:\jsr.sav   Save

Save as type: SPSS (*.sav)   Paste

☑ Write variable names to spreadsheet   Cancel

Box 2.9 **Save Data As** dialog box

name refers to the type of file. The default extension name for files in **Data Editor** is **sav**. Thus, we could call our data file **jsr.sav**. Extensions are now usually displayed as icons and not names (as shown in Box 2.10).

We shall generally use a particular notation throughout this book as shorthand to describe the steps involved in any application. The selection of a step or option will be indicated with a right facing-arrow → pointing to the term(s) on the menu or dialog box to be chosen. Any explanations will be placed in square parentheses after the option shown. Steps in a dialog box or a *subdialog* box (which is a box which can only be accessed after the initial dialog box has been opened) will begin on a new line. The sequence will be indented. Thus, the notation for saving this file on a floppy disk in Drive A is:

→**File** [shown in Box 2.8] →**Save As…** [opens **Save Data As** dialog box shown in Box 2.9]
type **a:\jsr.sav** in box beside **File name:** →**Save**

RETRIEVING A SAVED DATA EDITOR FILE

To retrieve this file at a later stage when it is no longer the current file, use the following procedure:

→**File** →**Open** [opens **Open File** dialog box shown in Box 2.10]
type **a:\jsr.sav** in box beside **File name:** →**Open**

READING AN ASCII DATA FILE IN DATA EDITOR

If the data have been saved on a floppy disk as an ASCII file called **jsr.dat**, then carry out the following sequence to put it in **Data Editor**:

→**File** →**Read Text Data…** [opens **Open File** dialog box shown in Box 2.10] type **a:\jsr.dat** in box beside **File name:** →**Open** [opens **Text Import Wizard – Step 1 of 6** dialog box shown in Box 2.11]
→**Next >** [opens **Text Import Wizard – Step 2 of 6** dialog box]
→**Fixed width** →**Next >** [opens **Text Import Wizard – Step 3 of 6** dialog box]
→**Next >** [opens **Text Import Wizard – Step 4 of 6** dialog box]
→**Next >** [opens **Text Import Wizard – Step 5 of 6** dialog box]
→**Next >** [opens **Text Import Wizard – Step 6 of 6** dialog box]
→**Finish** [closes **Text Import Wizard – Step 6 of 6** dialog box and displays data in **Data View**]
→**Variable View** [to define data]

STATISTICAL PROCEDURES

After entering the data set in **Data Editor**, we are now ready to analyse it. The rest of the book describes numerous ways in which you can do this. To show you how this is generally done, we shall ask SPSS to calculate the average or *mean* age of the sample. This can be done with a number of SPSS commands, but we shall use the one called **Descriptive Statistics.** This works out a number of other descriptive statistics as well. The procedure for doing this is:

→**Analyze** →**Descriptive Statistics** →**Descriptives...** [opens **Descriptives** dialog box shown in Box 2.12]
→variable [for example, **age**; note variables are listed in their order in **Data Editor**] →▶button [puts the selected variable in box under **Variable[s]:**] →**OK**

The output for this procedure is displayed in the **Viewer** window as shown in Table 2.3. The mean age is **39.19**. The other descriptive statistics provided by default are the standard deviation (see Chapter 5), the minimum age, the maximum age, and the number of cases (**N**) on which this information is based. If we look at the ages in our Job Survey data, we can confirm that the minimum age is indeed 18 (for the first case) while the maximum is 63 (for case number 5). We should also notice that the age of one of our participants (case number 45) is missing, making the number of cases which provide valid data for this variable 69 and not 70.

As shown in Table 2.3 the output in the **Viewer** window will always be preceded by the name of the statistical procedure. In this case, it is **Descriptives**. These titles will be omitted from subsequent presentations of output to save space.

If we wanted just the mean age and not the other statistics, we could do this

Box 2.10 **Open File** dialog box

Box 2.11 **Text Import Wizard - Step 1 of 6** dialog box

Box 2.12 **Descriptives** dialog box

Table 2.3 Default **Descriptives** output

Descriptive Statistics

	N	Minimum	Maximum	Mean	Std. Deviation
AGE	69	18	63	39.19	12.32
Valid N (listwise)	69				

as follows. Select **Options...** in the **Descriptives** dialog box to open the **Descriptives: Options** subdialog box shown in Box 2.13. Then de-select **Std. deviation**, **Minimum** and **Maximum** by moving the cursor on to them and pressing the left button. The output for this procedure is presented in Table 2.4.

If you want to revert to the **Data Editor**, either select **jsr – S...** at the bottom of the screen or select the **Window** option and then **1 jsr – SPSS Data Editor** from the drop-down menu. If an SPSS operation has been started but not completed (in that all dialog boxes concerned with that operation have not been closed), scrolling through the **Viewer** will not be possible.

SAVING AND PRINTING OUTPUT

To print the contents of any window, enter that window and then execute the following sequence:

→**File** →**Print...** →**OK**

If you want to store the contents of any window on a floppy disk, then carry out the following steps:

Box 2.13 **Descriptives: Options** subdialog box

Table 2.4 **Mean Descriptive** output

Descriptive Statistics

	N	Mean
AGE	69	39.19
Valid N (listwise)	69	

➔**File** ➔**Save As** ➔window [opens **Save As** dialog box]
➔type the drive and file name in the box beside **File name:** [for example,
a:\jsr.spo] ➔**Save**

The default extension name for output files is **spo** which is short for **sp**ss **o**utput
file. You can edit output files before saving them. For example, you may wish to
delete certain analyses or type in some further explanation.

HELP SYSTEM

SPSS has a **Help** system which you may like to use to avoid having to refer to a
book like this one or to find out more about the program. As this system is meant
to be self-explanatory you should be able to learn to use it yourself after a little
experience. To find help on a topic such as **file**, carry out the following procedure:

Box 2.14 **Help Topics Content** dialog box

→**Help** →**Topics** [opens **Help Topics Contents** window shown in Box 2.14]
→**Find** [opens **Help Topics Find** window shown in Box 2.15] →in first box
type in the appropriate or closest term [for example, **file**] →**Select some match-
ing topics to narrow your search** [for example, **File**] →**Click a topic, then
click Display** [for example, **Open file**] →**Display** [opens **Help** information box
shown in Box 2.16] →**?** [to **Mi<u>n</u>imise** or **<u>C</u>lose** the **Help** system]

If you want help while in a dialog box, select the **Help** option in the dialog box.

LEAVING SPSS

To leave SPSS, select **<u>F</u>ile** and then **E<u>x</u>it**. If you have edited or analysed data in a
session, you will be asked if you wish to save the contents in the **data editor** or
output viewer. If you don't, select **<u>N</u>o**. If you do, select **<u>Y</u>es** and name the file if
you have not already done so. This means, for example, that if you exit without
saving any changes that you may need to keep, those changes will be lost.

Box 2.15 **Help Topics Find** dialog box

Box 2.16 **Help** information box

EXERCISES

1   You need to collect information on the religious affiliation of your respond-
    ents. You have thought of the following options: Agnostic, Atheist, Buddhist,
    Catholic, Jewish, Hindu, Muslim, Protestant and Taoist. Which further
    category has to be included?
2   You want to record this information in a data file to be stored in a computer.
    How would you code this information?
3   Looking through your completed questionnaires, you notice that on one of
    them no answer has been given to this question. What are you going to put in
    your data file for this person?
4   Suppose that on another questionnaire the respondent had ticked two cate-
    gories. How would you deal with this situation?
5   The first two of your sample of fifty participants describe themselves as
    agnostic and the second two as atheists. The ages of these four participants are
    25, 47, 33, and 18. How would you arrange this information in your data file?
6   If data were available for all the options of the religious affiliation question,
    how many columns in an ASCII file would be needed to store this infor-
    mation?
7   How does SPSS know to what the numbers in the data file refer?
8   How many columns to a line are there in most computers for listing data?
9   What is the maximum number of characters that can be used for the name of a
    variable in SPSS?

APPENDIX 2.1: THE JOB SURVEY QUESTIONS

Employee questionnaire

This questionnaire is designed to find out a few things about yourself and your job.
Please answer the questions truthfully. There are no right or wrong answers.

		Code	Col
1	To which one of the following racial or ethnic groups do you belong?		
	(Tick one)		4
	__ White/European	1	
	__ Asian	2	
	__ West Indian	3	
	__ African	4	
	__ Other	5	
2	Are you male or female?		6
	Male	1	
	Female	2	
3	What is your current annual income before tax and other deductions?		
	£_____		8–12

4   What was your age last birthday (in years)?

                 __ years   14–15

5   How many years have you worked for this firm?

                 __ years   17–18

6   Please indicate whether you (1) strongly disagree, (2) disagree, (3) are un-decided, (4) agree, or (5) strongly agree with each of the following statements. Circle one answer only for each statement.

		SD	D	U	A	SA	
(a)	I would not leave this firm even if another employer could offer me a little more money	1	2	3	4	5	20
(b)	My job is like a hobby to me	1	2	3	4	5	22
(c)	Most of the time I have to force myself to go to work	1	2	3	4	5	24
(d)	Most days I am enthusiastic about my work	1	2	3	4	5	26
(e)	My job is pretty uninteresting	1	2	3	4	5	28
(f)	I am allowed to do my job as I choose	1	2	3	4	5	30
(g)	I am able to make my own decisions about how I do my job	1	2	3	4	5	32
(h)	People in my section of the firm are left to do their work as they please	1	2	3	4	5	34
(i)	I do not have to consult my supervisor if I want to perform my work slightly differently	1	2	3	4	5	36
(j)	I do my job in much the same way every day	1	2	3	4	5	38
(k)	There is little variety in my work	1	2	3	4	5	40
(l)	My job is repetitious	1	2	3	4	5	42
(m)	Very few aspects of my job change from day to day	1	2	3	4	5	44

7   Did you attend the firm's meeting this month?   46

                 __ Yes   1

                 __ No   2

Supervisor questionnaire

I should be grateful if you would answer the following questions about one of the people for whom you act as supervisor – [Name of employee]

1   Please describe the skill level of work that this person performs. Which one of the following descriptions best fits her/his work? (Tick one)   48

         __ Unskilled   1
         __ Semi-skilled   2
         __ Fairly skilled 3
         __ Highly skilled 4

2   How would you rate her/his productivity? (Tick one)   50
         __ Very poor   1
         __ Poor   2
         __ Average   3
         __ Good   4
         __ Very good   5

3   How would you rate the quality of her/his work? (Tick one)   52
         __ Very poor   1
         __ Poor   2
         __ Average   3
         __ Good   4
         __ Very good   5

4   How many days has s/he been absent in the last twelve months?
                         __ days   54–55

Chapter 3

Analysing data with computers

Further steps with SPSS 10 for Windows

Now that we have described how you generally set up and analyse a data file, we can introduce you to some further procedures which you may find very useful. These procedures will enable you to do the following: select certain cases (such as all white men under the age of 40) for separate analyses; and create new variables (such as scoring an attitude or personality scale) and new data files to store them. SPSS can also carry out other operations which are not described in this book, such as combining files in various ways. If you want to do things which are not mentioned here, then consult the Help system or SPSS Guide.

Box 3.1 **Select Cases** dialog box

Box 3.2 **Select Cases: If** subdialog box

SELECTING CASES

To choose cases with certain characteristics, you select **Data** and **Select Cases…** which opens the **Select Cases** dialog box shown in Box 3.1. If, for example, you wanted to find out the average age of only the men in the Job Survey sample, select **If condition is satisfied** and then **If…** which opens the **Select Cases: If** subdialog box presented in Box 3.2. In the empty box you enter the condition(s) cases must satisfy if they are to be selected. In this instance, we select in sequence **gender = 1** since men are coded **1**. We then select **Continue** to close the **Select Cases: If** subdialog box and **OK** to close the **Select Cases** dialog box.

To calculate just the mean age of men we carry out the following sequence:

→**Analyze** →**Descriptive Statistics** →**Descriptives…** [opens **Descriptives** dialog box shown in Box 2.12]
→**age** →▶button →**Options…** [opens the **Descriptives: Options** subdialog box shown in Box 2.13]
→**Std. deviation** [to de-select] →**Minimum** →**Maximum** →**Continue** →**OK**

The output from this procedure is presented in Table 3.1.

This selection will remain in force until you change it. If you want to carry out statistical analyses on the whole sample or on females, you need to alter the selec-

Table 3.1 Mean age of the men in the
Job Survey

Descriptive Statistics

	N	Mean
AGE	38	39.21
Valid N (listwise)	38	

tion. For analyses on the whole sample you would need to select **All cases** while for those on women you would have to enter the conditional expression **gender = 2**.

RELATIONAL OPERATORS

A relational operator such as = compares the value on its left (for example, **gender**) with that on its right (for example, **1**). There are six such operators, which are represented by the following symbols:

=   equal to
~=   not equal to
<   less than
<=   less than or equal to
>   greater than
>=   greater than or equal to

The question of which is the most appropriate operator to use in selecting cases will depend on the selection criteria. To select cases under 40 years of age, we could use less than (<):

age < 40

It would also, of course, have been possible to use less than or equal to (<=) 39 in this instance since we are dealing with whole numbers:

age <= 39

To select non-whites, we could use not equal to (~=) **1** since whites are coded **1**:

ethnicgp ~= 1

COMBINING LOGICAL RELATIONS

We can combine logical expressions with the logical operators **&** (**and**) and | (**or**). For example, we can select white men under 40 with the following conditional expression:

ethnicgp = 1 & gender = 1 & age < 40

To select people of only West Indian and African origin, we would have to use the | (**or**) logical operator:

ethnicgp = 3 | ethnicgp = 4

Note that it is necessary to repeat the full logical relation. It is *not* permissible to abbreviate this command as:

ethnicgp = 3 | 4

An alternative way of doing the same thing is to use the **any** logical function where any case with a value of either **3** or **4** for the variable **ethnicgp** is selected:

any (ethnicgp,3,4)

The variable and the values to be selected are placed in parentheses.

To select people between the ages of 30 and 40 inclusively, we can use the expression:

age >= 30 & age <= 40

Here, we have to use the **&** (**and**) logical operator. If we used | (**or**), we would in effect be selecting the whole sample since everybody is either above 30 or below 40 years of age.

Another way of selecting people aged 30 to 40 inclusively is to use the **range** logical function where any case with a value in the range of 30 to 40 for the variable **age** is selected:

range (age,30,40)

RECODING THE VALUES OF VARIABLES

Sometimes it is necessary to change or to recode the values of some variables. For example, it is recommended that the wording of questions which go to make up a scale or index should be varied in such a way that people who say yes to everything (*yeasayers*) or no (*naysayers*) do not end up with an extreme score. To illustrate this, we have worded two of the four questions assessing job satisfaction in the Job Survey ('6c. Most of the time I have to force myself to go to work' and '6e. My job is pretty uninteresting') in the opposite direction from the other two ('6b. My job is like a hobby to me' and '6d. Most days I am enthusiastic about my work'). These questions are answered in terms of a five-point scale ranging from 1 ('strongly disagree') to 5 ('strongly agree'). While we could reverse the numbers for the two negatively worded items (6c and 6e) on the questionnaire, this would draw the attention of our respondents to what we were trying to accomplish. It is simpler to reverse the coding when we come to analyse the data. Since we want to indicate greater job satisfaction with a higher number, we shall recode the answers to the two negatively worded questions, so that 1 becomes 5, 2 becomes 4, 4 becomes 2, and 5 becomes 1. We can do this with the **Recode** procedure which is on the

Recode into Different Variables   ☒

ethnicgp   Numeric Variable -> Output Variable: ┌Output Variable─
gender   satis2 --> rsatis2   Name:
income   satis4 --> ?
age   rsatis4   Change
years
commit   Label:
satis1
satis3
autonom1
autonom2   If...
autonom3
autonom4   Old and New Values...

                      OK   Paste   Reset   Cancel   Help

Box 3.3 **Recode into Different Variables** dialog box

<u>T</u>ransform menu. We can recode values using either the same (**Into <u>S</u>ame Variables...**) or different (**Into <u>D</u>ifferent Variables...**) variable names.

If we want to compare the original values with the recoded ones or if we want to retain the original values, we use the **Into <u>D</u>ifferent Variables...** option which opens the **Recode into Different Variables** dialog box presented in Box 3.3. For instance, if we wish to recode **satis2** and **satis4** into the respective two new variables of **rsatis2** and **rsatis4**, we select **satis2** which puts it in the box entitled **Numeric <u>V</u>ariable -> Output Variable:**, type the new variable name of **rsatis2** in the box entitled **<u>N</u>ame:** select **<u>C</u>hange** and repeat the procedure for **satis4**, renaming it **rsatis4**.

Then we select **<u>O</u>ld and New Values...** which opens the **Recode into Different Variables: Old and New Values** subdialog box displayed in Box 3.4. In the box entitled **<u>V</u>alue:** (in the **Old Value** section where the **V** of **<u>V</u>alue:** is underlined to distinguish it from **Value:** in the **New Value** section where the **l** of **Va<u>l</u>ue:** is underscored) we type the first value to be changed (for example, **1**) while in the box called **Va<u>l</u>ue:** (in the **New Value** section) we type the new value (for example, **5**) and select **<u>A</u>dd**. We do this consecutively for the three other old values of **2**, **4** and **5**. For the values which remain the same (for example, **3**) we can type the old value in the box called **Value:**, and select **Copy old value[s]** and **<u>A</u>dd**. The values for each case are recoded from left to right and are only changed once so that when 1 is initially recoded as 5 (**1 -> 5**) in the above example, it is not subsequently re-converted to 1 (**5 -> 1**). If there are missing values, as in this case, select **System- or user-missing** (in **Old Value** section) and **System-missing** (in **New Value** section).

After doing this we select **Continue** to close the **Recode into Different Variables: Old and New Values** subdialog box and **OK** to close the **Recode Into Different Variables** dialog box. We can then check the recoded values in the appropriate columns (**satis2**, **rsatis2**, **satis4** and **rsatis4**) in the **Data Editor**.

```
┌─────────────────────────────────────────────────────────────────────┐
│ Recode into Different Variables: Old and New Values          [X]      │
├─────────────────────────────────────────────────────────────────────┤
│  ┌─Old Value──────────────────┐   ┌─New Value────────────────────┐    │
│   ○ Value: [          ]           ○ Value: [       ]  ⊙ System-missing│
│   ○ System-missing                ○ Copy old value(s)                 │
│   ⊙ System- or user-missing              Old --> New:                 │
│   ○ Range:                      ┌─────────┐ ┌──────────────────────┐  │
│      [        ] through [     ]  │  Add    │ │ 1 --> 5              │  │
│                                  └─────────┘ │ 2 --> 4              │  │
│                                  ┌─────────┐ │ 3 --> Copy           │  │
│   ○ Range:                       │ Change  │ │ 4 --> 2              │  │
│      Lowest through [        ]   └─────────┘ │ 5 --> 1              │  │
│                                  ┌─────────┐ │ MISSING --> SYSMIS   │  │
│                                  │ Remove  │ └──────────────────────┘  │
│   ○ Range:                       └─────────┘                          │
│      [        ] through highest     □ Output variables are strings Width: [8]│
│                                     □ Convert numeric strings to numbers (5->5)│
│   ○ All other values             ┌────────┐ ┌────────┐ ┌────────┐     │
│                                  │Continue│ │ Cancel │ │  Help  │     │
│                                  └────────┘ └────────┘ └────────┘     │
└─────────────────────────────────────────────────────────────────────┘
```

Box 3.4 **Recode into Different Variables: Old and New Values** subdialog box

Alternatively, we can check the recoded values of **rsatis2** and **rsatis4** by selecting **Summarize Cases** and listing the values of **satis2**, **rsatis2**, **satis4** and **rsatis4** for, say, the first ten cases as shown in Table 3.2:

→**Analyze** →**Reports** →**Case Summaries...** [opens **Summarizes Cases** dialog box shown in Box 3.5]
→select variables [for example, **satis2**] →▶button →**Limit cases to first** and type number [for example, **10**]
→**OK**

Table 3.2 **Case Summaries** output showing recoded values of **rsatis2** and **rsatis4**

Case Summaries[a]

	SATIS2	RSATIS2	SATIS4	RSATIS4
1	3	3.00	4	2.00
2	0		3	3.00
3	4	2.00	1	5.00
4	5	1.00	4	2.00
5	4	2.00	1	5.00
6	5	1.00	3	3.00
7	3	3.00	3	3.00
8	2	4.00	2	4.00
9	1	5.00	4	2.00
10	2	4.00	3	3.00
Total N	9	9	10	10

[a]   Limited to first 10 cases.

Box 3.5 **Summarize Cases** dialog box

If we do not want to retain the original values, we select the **Into Same Variables...** option which opens the **Recode into Same Variables** dialog box presented in Box 3.6. For example, if we want to recode **satis2** and **satis4** we select them, which puts them in the box entitled **Variables:**.

We then proceed as previously by selecting **Old and New Values...** which opens the **Recode into Same Variables: Old and New Values** subdialog box displayed in Box 3.7. In the box entitled **Value:** (in the **Old Value** section) we type the first value to be changed (for example, **1**) while in the box called **Value:** (in the **New Value** section) we type the new value (for example, **5**) and select **Add**. We do this consecutively for the three other old values of **2**, **4** and **5**. We can also do this for **3**. If there are missing values, as in this case, select **System- or user-missing** (in **Old Value** section) and **System-missing** (in **New Value** section).

Alternatively, we can select **All other values**, type **3** in the box called **Value:** (in the **New Value** section) and select **Add**.

After doing this we select **Continue** to close the **Recode into Same Variables: Old and New Values** subdialog box and **OK** to close the **Recode into Same Variables** dialog box.

For each variable there can only be one new value, whereas there can be any number of old values. For example, if we wished to form a three-point scale with only one agree, one disagree, and one undecided answer, we could do this by recoding **1** and **2** into **1**, **3** into **2**, and **4** and **5** into **3**. Since only one value can be entered at a time into the box entitled **Value** we would have to do this sequentially. We can specify a range of old values by selecting the **Range:** option (which is distinguished by having the **n** of **Range:** underlined) and typing the lowest value in the first box and the highest value in the second box. For example, we could recode

Box 3.6 **Recode into Same Variables** dialog box

Box 3.7 **Recode into Same Variables: Old and New Values** subdialog box ethnic group into whites and non-whites by putting **3** into the first box and **5** into the second box and recoding **3** through **5** as **2**.

If we do not wish to find out what the lowest value is, we can specify it by selecting **Range:**. If we wanted to specify the highest value without determining what it was we would select **Range:**. For example, we could use these options to categorise our sample into those 40 years old or above and those below by recoding the **Lowest through 39** as **1** and the **40 through highest** as **2**.

If we had ages which were not whole numbers and which fell between 39 and 40, such as 39.9, they would not be recoded. To avoid this problem, we would use overlapping end-points so that **Lowest through 40** is recoded as **1** and **40 through highest** as **2**. In this example all people aged 40 and less would be coded as 1. Since values are recoded consecutively and once only, age 40 will not also be recoded as 2.

COMPUTING A NEW VARIABLE

Sometimes we want to create a new variable. For example, we have used four items to assess what may be slightly different aspects of job satisfaction. Rather than treat these items as separate measures, it may be preferable and reasonable to combine them into one index. To do this, we select the **Compute...** procedure on the **Transform** menu which displays the **Compute Variable** dialog box shown in Box 3.8. We can use this procedure to create a new variable called **satis** by adding together **satis1**, the recoded **rsatis2**, **satis3** and the recoded **rsatis4**. We do this by first typing the name of the new variable **satis** in the box entitled **Target Variable:**. Then, scrolling through the functions, we select **SUM(numexpr,**

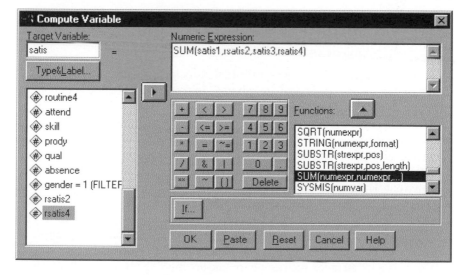

Box 3.8 **Compute Variable** dialog box

Table 3.3 **Case Summaries** output showing values of **satis1**,
rsatis2, **satis3**, **rsatis4** and **satis**

Case Summaries[a]

	SATIS1	RSATIS2	SATIS3	RSATIS4	SATIS
1	0	3.00	4	2.00	9.00
2	0		2	3.00	5.00
3	4	2.00	4	5.00	15.00
4	2	1.00	2	2.00	7.00
5	3	2.00	4	5.00	14.00
6	2	1.00	3	3.00	9.00
7	3	3.00	2	3.00	11.00
8	2	4.00	4	4.00	14.00
9	3	5.00	2	2.00	12.00
10	3	4.00	3	3.00	13.00
Total N	8	9	10	10	10

    [a] Limited to first 10 cases.

numexpr,...) which is entered into the box entitled **Numeric Expression:**. In this box we replace the **?,?** with **satis1,rsatis2,satis3,rsatis4** and then select **OK**. If the items had the same stem of **satis** and were listed sequentially, we need list only the first item (**satis1**) followed by **to** and the last item (**satis4**).

If we look at the value of **satis** in the **Data Editor** we see that it is **9.00** for the first case (**3+4+2=9.00**), **5.00** for the second case (**2+3=5.00**) and **15.00** for the third case (**4+2+4+5=15.00**). Once again, we could list the appropriate values for a selection of cases by using the **Case Summaries...** procedure. Table 3.3 shows the output for the first ten cases.

MISSING DATA AND COMPUTING SCORES TO FORM NEW MEASURES

As we have seen, the **satis1** score for the first participant and the **satis1** and **satis2** scores for the second participant are missing. In research, it is quite common for some scores to be missing. Participants may omit to answer questions; they may circle two different answers to the same question; the experimenter may forget to record a response, and so on. It is important to consider carefully how you are going to deal with missing data. If many of the data for one particular variable are missing, this suggests that there are problems with its measurement which need to be sorted out. Thus, for example, it may be a question which does not apply to most people, in which case it is best omitted. If many scores for an individual are missing, it is most probably best to omit this person from the sample since there may be problems with the way in which these data were collected. Thus, for example, it could be that the participant was not paying attention to the task at hand.

Where data for an index such as job routine are missing for some individuals, it is not appropriate to use the sum of the responses as an index since the total score will not reflect the same number of responses. For example, someone who answers 'strongly agree' (coded 5) to all four job routine items will have a total score of 20 whereas someone who strongly agrees with all items but who, for some reason, did not give an answer to one of them will have a total score of only 15. In other words, when we have missing data for items that constitute an index we need to take account of the missing data. In this situation a more appropriate index is the mean score of the non-missing values, which would be 5 for the first (20/4=5) and the second (15/3=5) individual. Another advantage of using the mean score for a scale such as job routine is that the mean score now corresponds to the answers to the individual items, so that an average score of 4.17 indicates that that person generally answers 'agree' to those items.

However, we would not generally want to derive an average score for someone who has a relatively large amount of data missing. A criterion sometimes applied to what constitutes too much missing data is: if more than 10 per cent of the data are missing for an index, then the index itself is defined as missing for that participant. If we applied this principle to the two participants in the Job Survey, no score for job satisfaction would be computed for them, although they would have scores for job routine and autonomy.

To compute a mean score we use the **MEAN(numexpr,numexpr,…)** function in the **Compute Variable** dialog box. If we want to specify a minimum number of values that must be non-missing for the mean to be produced we type a full stop after **MEAN** followed by the minimum number. We shall use the four **satis** items to illustrate how this is done. With only four items, we cannot use a cut-off point of more than 10 per cent for exclusion as missing. Therefore, we shall adopt a more lenient criterion of more than 50 per cent. If more than 50 per cent (that is, two or more) of the scores for the job satisfaction items are missing, we shall code that variable for participants as missing. In other words, the minimum number of values that must be non-missing for the mean to be computed is 3. As before, the new variable is called **satis** but the numeric expression in the **Numeric Expression:** is **MEAN.3(satis1,rsatis2,satis3,rsatis4)**. If we examine the new values of **satis** in the **Data Editor** we see that it is **3.00** for the first case (**9.00/3=3.00**), . for the second case (since there are only two valid values) and **3.75** for the third case (**15.00/4=3.75**).

To display the mean value as a zero when it is missing, we use the **Recode into Same Variables** procedure in which we select **System-missing** in the box called **Old Value** and enter **0** in the box called **Value:** (in the **New Value** section) and select **Add**.

To convert this mean score back into a total score (which takes into account numbers of valid scores that might vary between three and four), we simply multiply this mean by the maximum number of items, which is 4. To do this we use the **Compute Variable** procedure where the new variable is still called **satis** and where the numeric expression is **satis*4**.

Since we wish to form three new variables (job satisfaction, job autonomy and job routine), we have to repeat this **Compute Variable** procedure for the job routine and job autonomy items. Although we know there are no missing values for these two sets of variables, it does no harm to be cautious and assume there may be some, as we have done. To determine if there are any rogue or missing values in data sets with which we are unfamiliar, we use the **Frequencies** procedure (see Chapter 5).

Aggregate measures of job satisfaction, job autonomy and job routine used in subsequent chapters have been based on summing the four items within each scale and assigning the summed score as missing where more than 10 per cent of the items were missing. Since two of the seventy cases in the Job Survey had one or two of the answers to the individual job satisfaction items missing, the number of cases for whom a summed job satisfaction score could be computed is 68. The summed scores for job satisfaction, job autonomy and job routine have been called **satis**, **autonom** and **routine** respectively. To do this for **satis**, for example, we first compute the mean score with the numeric expression **MEAN.4(satis1 to satis4)** and then convert this to a total score with the numeric expression **satis*4**.

When we have a data set that has a large number of variables which we may not need for a particular set of analyses, we may find it more convenient to create a new file which contains only those variables that we are going to examine. For example, if we intend to analyse the aggregate variables of **satis**, **routine** and **autonom** and not the individual items that constitute them, then we can create a new file which holds these new variables (together with any of the other variables we need) but which does not contain the individual items. We delete the individual items by selecting the variable names **satis1** to **routine4** in the **Data Editor** and selecting **Edit** and **Cut**. We then save the data in the **Data Editor** in a new file which we will call **'jssd.sav'** (for **j**ob **s**cored **s**urvey **d**ata) and which we will use in subsequent analyses. The data in this file are presented in Table 3.4.

EXERCISES

1   What is the SPSS procedure for selecting men and women of African origin in the Job Survey data?
2   Write the conditional expression for SPSS to select women of Asian or West Indian origin who are 25 years old or younger in the Job Survey data.
3   What is the conditional expression for selecting participants who had no missing job satisfaction scores in the Job Survey data?
4   What is the SPSS procedure for recoding the Job Survey variable **skill** into the same variable but with only two categories (unskilled/semi-skilled vs fairly/highly skilled).
5   What is the SPSS procedure for recoding the variable **income** into the new variable of **incomec** comprising three groups of those earning less than £5,000, between £5,000 and under £10,000, and £10,000 and over, and where missing values are assigned as zero?
6   Using the arithmetic operator *, express the variable **weeks** as **days**. In other words, convert the number of weeks into the number of days.

Table 3.4 The scored Job Survey data

id	ethnicgp	gender	income	age	years	commit	satis	autonom	routine	attend	skill	prody	qual	absence
1	1	1	16600	29	1	4	0	10	9	2	3	0	1	7
2	2	1	14600	26	5	2	0	7	15	1	3	4	4	8
3	3	1	17800	40	5	4	15	7	8	1	4	3	4	0
4	3	1	16400	46	15	2	7	7	10	2	3	3	4	4
5	2	2	18600	63	36	4	14	11	18	1	3	5	3	0
6	1	1	16000	54	31	2	9	6	16	1	-	3	4	-
7	1	1	16600	29	2	0	11	9	14	2	3	5	2	0
8	3	1	17600	35	2	5	14	12	11	2	3	4	4	2
9	2	2	17600	33	4	3	12	10	9	2	2	-	-	5
10	2	2	13800	27	6	4	13	8	15	1	2	2	4	4
11	1	2	14200	29	4	2	7	6	16	2	2	2	3	8
12	2	1	0	19	2	-	6	4	13	-	3	2	3	4
13	4	1	18000	55	35	3	14	9	19	-	4	3	5	-
14	1	2	17000	29	1	2	9	8	15	-	-	2	2	0
15	3	1	18200	48	8	3	14	13	11	2	4	5	5	-
16	2	1	15800	32	7	3	11	8	10	2	2	2	3	4
17	1	1	16600	48	14	3	10	7	17	-	2	5	3	-
18	1	2	13400	18	-	2	8	9	16	-	2	3	3	6
19	3	2	15000	28	2	4	15	13	10	2	3	4	4	3
20	3	2	17600	37	-	3	11	8	18	-	-	4	-	3
21	1	1	0	43	16	-	12	11	13	2	4	5	2	6
22	1	1	17400	39	6	3	10	10	15	2	-	-	5	5
23	1	1	18000	53	5	-	13	11	14	-	3	3	5	13
24	2	2	16000	34	9	-	7	5	14	2	-	3	3	9
25	3	2	17000	43	17	4	13	9	13	-	3	5	2	2
26	1	1	14000	21	-	4	13	14	9	-	2	5	5	3
27	1	1	16200	50	28	3	10	6	19	-	2	2	4	8
28	1	2	12400	31	9	-	6	7	17	2	3	5	5	0

continued

Table 3.4 continued

29	—	—	13600	31	12	3	11	10	8	1	3	3	4	6
30	2	2	16400	52	21	2	14	12	8	2	4	5	3	10
31	—	1	14400	54	12	3	14	10	15	2	4	4	2	99
32	3	2	12400	28	10	2	6	7	11	—	2	4	4	9
33	2	2	16600	50	23	4	14	13	12	2	3	4	5	5
34	2	2	16000	52	21	5	13	13	10	—	3	2	5	4
35	—	2	15000	40	21	—	11	10	9	—	2	2	3	6
36	2	—	11800	19	1	2	7	7	20	2	2	3	2	3
37	2	—	17600	38	4	5	16	14	6	2	4	4	4	8
38	2	—	18000	61	41	5	16	9	7	2	3	5	4	3
39	—	2	15600	37	8	3	9	10	18	—	3	4	4	8
40	2	—	13400	31	5	2	6	7	19	2	—	1	2	5
41	2	2	15000	43	21	4	13	12	12	—	—	4	2	0
42	3	—	13600	23	3	—	7	5	17	—	3	2	2	8
43	2	2	14000	27	5	—	6	5	17	2	—	2	1	9
44	—	—	15000	28	7	3	14	14	6	—	2	4	3	9
45	3	—	13200	0	10	4	6	8	16	—	4	—	3	9
46	—	2	13400	18	1	3	13	9	16	—	4	3	4	10
47	—	2	20600	48	23	2	13	9	8	—	4	4	4	3
48	—	2	13600	29	10	2	10	7	11	2	3	4	4	8
49	—	—	14600	42	10	4	11	7	20	—	4	4	4	11
50	2	—	18200	53	12	3	19	16	8	2	—	4	4	0
51	—	—	15200	32	12	—	7	10	12	2	4	3	4	1
52	—	2	13000	31	2	5	6	9	18	—	2	3	2	1
53	—	—	19000	55	19	4	15	15	13	2	—	4	1	8
54	3	2	14800	26	8	3	15	14	6	—	3	3	3	0
55	—	2	17200	53	22	2	16	14	7	2	4	5	5	2
56	—	—	15600	51	31	3	12	13	19	—	3	—	1	0
57	—	—	15400	48	23	—	8	8	19	—	4	3	2	8
58	2	2	13800	48	28	1	5	7	20	2	—	4	3	6

continued

Table 3.4 continued

59	2	2	15800	62	40	1	8	9	18	2	1	1	5	7
60	2	1	17400	57	13	2	10	8	13	1	4	4	1	4
61	1	2	17800	42	20	5	14	12	9	2	3	3	3	2
62	3	1	14200	21	2	—	8	8	12	1	4	2	2	0
63	3	2	12800	26	8	3	8	5	10	2	4	1	1	4
64	1	2	13600	46	0	1	7	8	20	2	2	3	4	5
65	4	2	21000	59	21	4	15	10	9	2	4	5	1	4
66	1	2	14200	30	8	0	10	9	17	1	2	2	3	2
67	1	—	14600	29	8	3	12	8	15	2	1	4	5	10
68	3	—	13800	45	9	2	10	12	13	2	2	3	4	9
69	3	—	16000	53	30	3	10	7	16	2	2	1	4	2
70	1	—	13800	47	22	2	8	11	16	1	2	4	4	11

Chapter 4

Concepts and their measurement

Concepts form a linchpin in the process of social research. Hypotheses contain concepts which are the products of our reflections on the world. Concepts express common elements in the world to which we give a name. We may notice that some people have an orientation in which they dislike people of a different race from their own, often attributing to other races derogatory characteristics. Still others are highly supportive of racial groups, perhaps seeing them as enhancing the 'host' culture through instilling new elements into it and hence enriching it. Yet others are merely tolerant, having no strong views one way or the other about people of other racial groups. In other words, we get a sense that people exhibit a variety of positions in regard to racial groups. We may want to suggest that there is a common theme to these attitudes, even though the attitudes themselves may be mutually antagonistic. What seems to bind these dispositions together is that they reflect different positions in regard to 'racial prejudice'. In giving a name to the various dispositions that may be held regarding persons of another race, we are treating it as a concept, an entity over and above the observations about racial hostility and supportiveness that prompted the formulation of a name for those observations. Racial prejudice has acquired a certain abstractness, so that it transcends the reflections that prompted its formulation. Accordingly, the concept of racial prejudice becomes something that others can use to inform their own reflections about the social world. In this way, hypotheses can be formulated which postulate connections between racial prejudice and other concepts, such as that it will be related to social class or to authoritarianism.

Once formulated, a concept and the concepts with which it is purportedly associated, such as social class and authoritarianism, will need to be *operationally defined*, in order for systematic research to be conducted in relation to it. An operational definition specifies the procedures (operations) that will permit differences between individuals in respect of the concept(s) concerned to be precisely specified. What we are in reality talking about here is *measurement*, that is, the assignment of numbers to the units of analysis – be they people, organisations, or nations – to which a concept refers. Measurement allows small differences between units to be specified. We can say that someone who actively speaks out against members of other races is racially prejudiced, while someone who actively supports them is the obverse of this, but it is difficult to specify precisely the different positions that people may hold in between these extremes. Measurement assists in the specification of such differences by allowing systematic differences between people to be stipulated.

In order to provide operational definitions of concepts, *indicators* are required which will stand for those concepts. It may be that a single indicator will suffice in the measurement of a concept, but in many instances it will not. For example, would it be sufficient to measure 'religious commitment' by conducting a survey in which people are asked how often they attend church services? Clearly it would not, since church attendance is but one way in which an individual's commitment to his or her religion may be expressed. It does not cover personal devotions, behaving as a religious person should in secular activities, being knowledgeable about one's faith, or how far they adhere to central tenets of faith (Glock and Stark, 1965). These reflections strongly imply that more than one indicator is likely to be required to measure many concepts; otherwise our findings may be open to the argument that we have tapped only one facet of the concept in question.

If more than one indicator of a concept can be envisaged, it may be necessary to test hypotheses with each of the indicators. Imagine a hypothesis in which 'organisational size' was a concept. We might measure (that is, operationally define) this concept by the number of employees in a firm, its turnover or its net assets. While these three prospective indicators are likely to be interconnected, they will not be perfectly related (Child, 1973), so that hypotheses about organisational size may need to be tested for each of the indicators. Similarly, if religious commitment is to be measured, it may be necessary to employ indicators which reflect all the facets of such commitment in addition to church attendance. For example, individuals may be asked how far they endorse central aspects of their faith in order to establish how far they adhere to the beliefs associated with their faith.

When questionnaires are employed to measure concepts, as in the case of religious commitment, researchers often favour multiple-item measures. In the Job Survey data, **satis** is an example of a multiple-item measure. It entails asking individuals their positions in relation to a number of indicators which stand for one concept. Similarly, there are four indicators of both **autonom** and **routine**. One could test a hypothesis with each of the indicators. However, if one wanted to use the Job Survey data to examine a hypothesis relating to **satis** and **autonom**, each of which contains four questions, sixteen separate tests would be required. The procedure for analysing such multiple-item measures is to aggregate each individual's response in relation to each question and to treat the overall measure as a scale in relation to which each unit of analysis has a score. In the case of **satis**, **autonom** and **routine**, the scaling procedure is *Likert scaling*, which is a popular approach to the creation of multiple-item measures. With Likert scaling, individuals are presented with a number of statements which appear to relate to a common theme; they then indicate their degree of agreement or disagreement on a five- or seven-point range. The answer to each constituent question (often called an *item*) is scored, for example from 1 for strongly disagree to 5 for strongly agree if the range of answers is in terms of five points. The individual scores are added up to form an overall score for each respondent. Multiple-item scales can be very long; the four **satis** questions are taken from an often-used scale developed by Brayfield and Rothe (1951) which comprised eighteen questions.

These multiple-item scales are popular for various reasons. First, a number of items are more likely to capture the totality of a broad concept like job satisfaction than a single question. Second, we can draw finer distinctions between people. The **satis** measure comprises four questions which are scored from 1 to 5, so that respondents' overall scores can vary between 4 and 20. If only one question was asked, the variation would be between 1 and 5 – a considerably narrower range of potential variation. Third, if a question is misunderstood by a respondent, when only one question is asked that respondent will not be appropriately classified; if a few questions are asked, a misunderstood question can be offset by those which are properly understood.

It is common to speak of measures as *variables*, to denote the fact that units of analysis differ in respect to the concept in question. If there is no variation in a measure, it is a *constant*. It is fairly unusual to find concepts whose measures are constants. On the whole, the social sciences are concerned with variables and with expressing and analysing the variation that variables exhibit. When *univariate analysis* is carried out, we want to know how individuals are distributed in relation to a single variable. For example, we may want to know how many cases can be found in each of the categories or levels of the measure in question, or we may be interested in what the average response is, and so on. With *bivariate analysis* we are interested in the connections between two variables at a time. For example, we may want to know whether the variation in **satis** is associated with variation in another variable like **autonom** or whether men and women differ in regard to **satis**. In each case, it is variation that is of interest.

TYPES OF VARIABLE

One of the most important features of an understanding of statistical operations is an appreciation of when it is permissible to employ particular tests. Central to this appreciation is an ability to recognise the different forms that variables take, because statistical tests presume certain kinds of variable, a point that will be returned to again and again in later chapters.

The majority of writers on statistics draw upon a distinction developed by Stevens (1946) between nominal, ordinal and interval/ratio scales or levels of measurement. First, *nominal* (sometimes called *categorical*) scales entail the classification of individuals in terms of a concept. In the Job Survey data, the variable **ethnicgp**, which classifies respondents in terms of five categories – white, Asian, West Indian, African and Other – is an example of a nominal variable. Individuals can be allocated to each category, but the measure does no more than this and there is not a great deal more that we can say about it as a measure. We cannot order the categories in any way, for example.

This inability contrasts with *ordinal* variables, in which individuals are categorised but the categories can be ordered in terms of 'more' and 'less' of the concept in question. In the Job Survey data, **skill**, **prody** and **qual** are all ordinal variables. If we take the first of these, **skill**, we can see that people are not merely categorised into each of four categories – highly skilled, fairly skilled, semi-skilled and unskilled – since we can see that someone who is fairly skilled is at a higher point on the scale than someone who is semi-skilled. We cannot make the same inference with **ethnicgp** since we cannot order the categories that it comprises. Although we can order the categories comprising **skill**, we are still limited in the things that we can say about it. For example, we cannot say that the skill difference between being highly skilled and fairly skilled is the same as the skill difference between being fairly skilled and semi-skilled. All we can say is that those rated as highly skilled have more skill than those rated as fairly skilled, who in turn have greater skill than the semi-skilled, and so on. Moreover, in coding semi-skilled as 2 and highly skilled as 4, we cannot say that people rated as highly skilled are twice as skilled as those rated as semi-skilled. In other words, care should be taken in attributing to the categories of an ordinal scale an arithmetic quality that the scoring seems to imply.

With *interval/ratio variables*, we can say quite a lot more about the arithmetic qualities. In fact, this category subsumes two types of variable – interval and ratio. Both types exhibit the quality that differences between categories are identical. For example, someone aged 20 is one year older than someone aged 19, and someone aged 50 is one year older than someone aged 49. In each case, the difference between the categories is identical – one year. A scale is called an interval scale because the intervals between categories are identical. Ratio measures have a fixed zero point. Thus age, absence and income have logical zero points. This quality means that one can say that somebody who is aged 40 is twice as old as someone aged 20. Similarly, someone who has been absent from work six times in a year has been absent three times as often as someone who has been absent twice. However, the distinction between interval and ratio scales is often not examined by writers because, in the social sciences, true interval variables frequently are also ratio variables (for example, income, age). In this book, the term *interval variable* will sometimes be employed to embrace ratio variables as well.

Interval/ratio variables are recognised to be the highest level of measurement because there is more that can be said about them than about the other two types. Moreover, a wider variety of statistical tests and procedures are available to interval/ratio variables. It should be noted that if an interval/ratio variable such as age is grouped into categories – such as 20–29, 30–39, 40–49, 50–59 and so on – it becomes an ordinal variable. We cannot really say that the difference between someone in the 40–49 group and someone in the 50–59 is the same as the difference between someone in the 20–29 group and someone in the 30–39 group, since we no longer know the points within the groupings at which people are located. On the other hand, such groupings of individuals are sometimes useful for the presentation and easy assimilation of information. It should be noted too that the position of *dichotomous* variables within the three-fold classification of types of variable is somewhat ambiguous. With such variables, there are only two categories, such as male and female for the variable gender. A dichotomy is usually thought of as a nominal variable, but sometimes it can be considered an ordinal variable. For example, when there is an inherent ordering to the dichotomy, such as passing and failing, the characteristics of an ordinal variable seem to be present.

Strictly speaking, measures like **satis**, **autonom** and **routine**, which derive from multiple-item scales, are ordinal variables. For example, we do not know whether the difference between a score of 20 on the **satis** scale and a score of 18 is the same as the difference between 10 and 8. This poses a problem for researchers since the inability to treat such variables as interval means that methods of analysis like correlation and regression (see Chapter 8), which are both powerful and popular, could not be used in their connection since these techniques presume the employment of interval variables. On the other hand, most of the multiple-item measures created by researchers are treated by them as though they were interval variables because these measures permit a large number of categories to be stipulated. When a variable allows only a small number of ordered categories, as in the case of **commit**, **prody**, **skill** and **qual** in the Job Survey data, each of which comprises only either four or five categories, it would be unreasonable in most analysts' eyes to treat them as interval variables. When the number of categories is considerably greater, as in the case of **satis**, **autonom** and **routine**, each of which can assume

Table 4.1 Types of variable

Type	Description	Example in Job Survey data
Nominal (categorical)	A classification of objects (people, firms, nations, etc.) into discrete categories that cannot be rank ordered.	**ethnicgp**
Ordinal	The categories associated with an ordinal variable that can be rank ordered. Objects can be ordered in terms of a criterion from highest to lowest.	**commit** **skill** **prody** **qual**
Interval (a)	With 'true' interval variables, categories associated with a variable can be rank ordered, as with an ordinal variable, but the distances between the categories are equal.	**income** **age** **years** **absence**
Interval (b)	Variables which strictly speaking are ordinal, but which have a large number of categories, such as multiple-item questionnaire measures. These variables are assumed to have similar properties to 'true' interval variables.	**satis** **routine** **autonom**
Dichotomous	A variable that comprises only two categories	**gender** **attend**

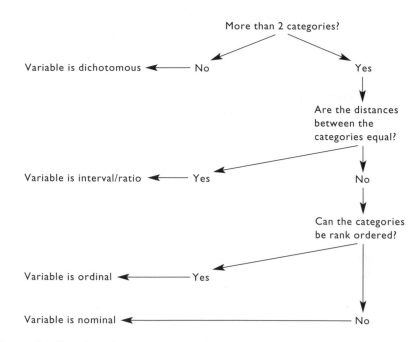

Figure 4.1 Deciding the nature of a variable

sixteen categories from 5 to 20, the case for treating them as interval variables is more compelling.

Certainly, there seems to be a trend in the direction of this more liberal treatment of multiple-item scales as having the qualities of an interval variable. On the other hand, many purists would demur from this position. Moreover, there does not appear to be a rule of thumb which allows the analyst to specify when a variable is definitely ordinal and when interval. None the less, in this book it is proposed to reflect much of current practice and to treat multiple-item measures such as **satis**, **autonom** and **routine** as though they were interval scales. Labovitz (1970) goes further in suggesting that almost all ordinal variables can and should be treated as interval variables. He argues that the amount of error that can occur is minimal, especially in relation to the considerable advantages that can accrue to the analyst as a result of using techniques of analysis like correlation and regression which are both powerful and relatively easy to interpret. However, this view is controversial (Labovitz, 1971) and whereas many researchers would accept the treatment of variables like **satis** as interval, they would cavil about variables like **commit**, **skill**, **prody** and **qual**. Table 4.1 summarises the main characteristics of the types of scale discussed in this section, along with examples from the Job Survey data.

In order to help with the identification of whether variables should be classified as nominal, ordinal, dichotomous, or interval/ratio, the steps articulated in Figure 4.1 can be followed. We can take some of the job survey variables to illustrate how this table can be used. First, we can take **skill**. This variable has more than two categories; the distances between the categories are not equal; the categories *can* be rank ordered; therefore the variable is ordinal. Now **income**. This variable has more than two categories; the distances between them are equal; therefore the variable is interval/ratio. Now **gender**. This variable does not have more than two categories; therefore it is dichotomous. Finally, we can take **ethnicgp**. This variable has more than two categories; the distances between the categories are not equal; the categories cannot be rank ordered; therefore, the variable is nominal.

DIMENSIONS OF CONCEPTS

When a concept is very broad, serious consideration needs to be given to the possibility that it comprises underlying dimensions which reflect different aspects of the concept in question. Very often it is possible to specify those dimensions on a priori grounds, so that possible dimensions are established in advance of the formation of indicators of the concept. There is much to recommend deliberation about the possibility of such underlying dimensions, since it encourages systematic reflection on the nature of the concept that is to be measured.

Lazarsfeld's (1958) approach to the measurement of concepts viewed the search for underlying dimensions as an important ingredient. Figure 4.2 illustrates the steps that he envisaged. Initially, the researcher forms an image from a theoretical domain. This image reflects a number of common characteristics, as in the previous example of job satisfaction which denotes the tendency for people to have a distinctive range of experiences in relation to their jobs. Similarly, Hall (1968) developed the idea of 'professionalism' as a consequence of his view that members of professions have a distinctive constellation of attitudes to the nature of their work. In each case, out of this *imagery* stage, we see a concept starting to form. At the next stage, *concept specification* takes place, whereby the concept is developed to show whether it comprises different aspects or dimensions. This stage allows the complexity of the concept to be recognised. In Hall's case, five dimensions of professionalism were proposed:

1   *The use of the professional organisation as a major reference* This means that the professional organisation and other members of the profession are the chief source of ideas and judgements for the professional in the context of his or her work.
2   *A belief in service to the public* According to this aspect, the profession is regarded as indispensable to society.
3   *Belief in self-regulation* This notion implies that the work of a professional can and should only be judged by other members of the profession, because only they are qualified to make appropriate judgements.
4   *A sense of calling to the field* The professional is someone who is dedicated to his or her work and would probably want to be a member of the profession even if material rewards were less.

Figure 4.2 Concepts, dimensions and measurements
        Sources: Lazarsfeld (1958); Hall (1968); Snizek (1972)

5   *Autonomy* This final dimension suggests that professionals ought to be able to make decisions and judgements without pressure from either clients, the organisations in which they work, or any other non-members of the profession.

Not only is the concept specification stage useful in order to reflect and to capture the full complexity of concepts, but it also serves as a means of bridging the general formulation of concepts and their measurement, since the establishment of dimensions reduces the abstractness of concepts.

The next stage is the *selection of indicators*, in which the researcher searches for indicators of each of the dimensions. In Hall's case, ten indicators of each dimension were selected. Each indicator entailed a statement in relation to which respondents had to answer whether they believed that it agreed very well, well, poorly, or very poorly in the light of how they felt and behaved as members of their profession. A neutral category was also provided. Figure 4.2 provides both the five dimensions of professionalism and one of the ten indicators for each dimension. Finally, Lazarsfeld proposed that the indicators need to be brought together through the *formation of indices* or *scales*. This stage can entail either of two possibilities: an overall scale could be formed comprising all indicators relating to all dimensions; or, more frequently, separate scales can be formulated for each dimension. Thus, in Hall's research, the indicators relating to each dimension were combined to form scales, so that we end up with five separate scales of professionalism. As Hall shows, different professions exhibit different 'profiles' in respect of these dimensions: one may emerge as having high scores for dimensions 2, 3, and 5, moderate for 1, and low for 4, whereas other professions will emerge with different combinations.

In order to check whether the indicators bunch in the ways proposed by an a priori specification of dimensions, *factor analysis*, a technique that will be examined in Chapter 11, is often employed. Factor analysis allows the researcher to check whether, for example, all of the ten indicators developed to measure 'autonomy' are really related to each other and not to indicators that are supposed to measure other dimensions. We might find that an indicator which is supposed to measure autonomy seems to be associated with many of the various indicators of 'belief in service to the public', while one or two of the latter might be related to indicators which are supposed to denote 'belief in self-regulation', and so on. In fact, when such factor analysis has been conducted in relation to Hall's professionalism scale, the correspondence between the five dimensions and their putative indicators has been shown to be poor (Snizek, 1972; Bryman, 1985). However, the chief point that should be recognised in the foregoing discussion is that the specification of dimensions for concepts is often an important step in the development of an operational definition.

Some measurement is carried out in psychology and sociology with little (if any) attention to the quest for dimensions of concepts. For example, the eighteen-item measure of job satisfaction developed by Brayfield and Rothe (1951), which was mentioned above, does not specify dimensions, though it is possible to employ factor analysis to search for de facto ones. The chief point that can be gleaned from this section is that the search for dimensions can provide an important aid to understanding the nature of concepts and that when established on the basis of a priori reasoning can be an important step in moving from the complexity and abstractness of many concepts to possible measures of them.

VALIDITY AND RELIABILITY OF MEASURES

It is generally accepted that when a concept has been operationally defined, in that a measure of it has been proposed, the ensuing measurement device should be both reliable and valid.

Reliability

The reliability of a measure refers to its consistency. This notion is often taken to entail two separate aspects: external and internal reliability. External reliability is the more common of the two meanings and refers to the degree of consistency of a measure over time. If you have kitchen scales which register a different weight every time the same bag of sugar is weighed, you would have an externally unreliable measure of weight, since the amount fluctuates over time in spite of the fact that there should be no differences between the occasions that the item is weighed. Similarly, if you administered a personality test to a group of people, readministered it shortly afterwards and found a poor correspondence between the two *waves* of measurement, the personality test would probably be regarded as externally unreliable because it seems to fluctuate. When assessing external reliability in this manner, that is by administering a test on two occasions to the same group of subjects, *test–retest reliability* is being examined. We would anticipate that people who scored high on the test initially will also do so when retested; in other words, we would expect the relative position of each person's score to remain comparatively constant. The problem with such a procedure is that intervening events between the test and the retest may account for any discrepancy between the two sets of results. For example, if the job satisfaction of a group of workers is gauged and three months later is reassessed, it might be found that in general respondents exhibit higher levels of satisfaction than previously. It may be that in the intervening period they have received a pay increase or a change to their working practices or some grievance that had been simmering before has been resolved by the time job satisfaction is retested. Also, if the test and retest are too close in time, subjects may recollect earlier answers, so that an artificial consistency between the two tests is created. However, test–retest reliability is one of the main ways of checking external reliability.

Internal reliability is particularly important in connection with multiple-item scales. It raises the question of whether each scale is measuring a single idea and hence whether the items that make up the scale are internally consistent. A number of procedures for estimating internal reliability exist, two of which can be readily computed in SPSS. First, with *split-half reliability* the items in a scale are divided into two groups (either randomly or on an odd–even basis) and the relationship between respondents' scores for the two halves is computed. Thus, the Brayfield–Rothe job satisfaction measure, which contains eighteen items, would be divided into two groups of nine, and the relationship between respondents' scores for the two halves would be estimated. A correlation coefficient is then generated (see Chapter 8), which varies between 0 and 1 and the nearer the result is to 1 – and preferably at or over 0.8 – the more internally reliable is the scale. Second, the currently widely used *Cronbach's alpha* essentially calculates the average of all possible split-half reliability coefficients. Again, the rule of thumb is that the result should be 0.8 or above. This rule of thumb is also generally used in relation to test–retest reliability. When a concept and its associated measure are deemed to comprise underlying dimensions, it is normal to calculate reliability estimates for each of the constituent dimensions rather than for the measure as a whole. Indeed, if a factor analysis confirms that a measure comprises a number of dimensions the overall scale will probably exhibit a low level of internal reliability, since the split-half reliability estimates may be lower as a result.

Box 4.1 **Reliability Analysis** dialog box

Both split-half and alpha estimates of reliability can be easily calculated with SPSS. It is necessary to ensure that all items are coded in the same direction. Thus, in the case of **satis** it is necessary to ensure that the reverse items (**satis2** and **satis4**) have been recoded (using **Recode**) so that agreement is indicative of job satisfaction. These two items have been recoded in the following illustration as **rsatis2** and **rsatis4**. In order to generate a reliability test of the four items that make up **satis**, the following sequence would be used:

→**Analyze** →**Scale** →**Reliability Analysis...** [opens **Reliability Analysis** dialog box shown in Box 4.1]
→**satis1**, **rsatis2**, **satis3** and **rsatis4** while holding down the Ctrl button [all four of the variables should be highlighted] →►button [puts **satis1**, **rsatis2**, **satis3** and **rsatis4** in the **Items:** box] →**Model:** →**Alpha** in the drop-down menu that appears
→**OK**

If split-half reliability testing is preferred, click on **Split-half** in the **Model:** pull-down menu rather than **Alpha**. The output for alpha (Table 4.2) suggests that **satis** is in fact internally reliable since the coefficient is 0.76. This is only just short of

Table 4.2 **Reliability Analysis** output for **satis** (Job Survey data)

```
R E L I A B I L I T Y    A N A L Y S I S    —    S C A L E    (A L P H A)

   Reliability Coefficients

   N of Cases =      68.0              N of Items =   4

   Alpha =     .7618
```

the 0.8 criterion and would be regarded as internally reliable for most purposes. If a scale turns out to have low internal reliability, a strategy for dealing with this eventuality is to drop one item or more from the scale in order to establish whether reliability can be boosted. To do this, select the **→Statistics...** button in the **Reliability Analysis** dialog box. This brings up the **Reliability Analysis: Statistics** subdialog box (shown in Box 4.2). Then **→Scale if item deleted**. The output shows the alpha reliability levels when each constituent item is deleted. Of course, in the case of **satis**, this exercise would not be necessary.

Two other aspects of reliability, that is in addition to internal and external reliability, ought to be mentioned. First, when material is being coded for themes, the reliability of the coding scheme should be tested. This problem can occur when a researcher needs to code people's answers to interview questions that have not been pre-coded in order to search for general underlying themes to answers, or when a content analysis of newspaper articles is conducted to elucidate ways in which news topics tend to be handled. When such exercises are carried out, more than one coder should be used and an estimate of *inter-coder reliability* should be provided to ensure that the coding scheme is being consistently interpreted by coders. This exercise would entail gauging the degree to which coders agree on the coding of themes deriving from the material being examined. Second, when the

Box 4.2 **Reliability Analysis: Statistics** subdialog box

researcher is classifying behaviour an estimate of *inter-observer reliability* should be provided. For example, if aggressive behaviour is being observed, an estimate of inter-observer reliability should be presented to ensure that the criteria of aggressiveness are being consistently interpreted. Methods of bivariate analysis (see Chapter 8) can be used to measure inter-coder and inter-observer reliability. A discussion of some methods which have been devised specifically for the assessment of inter-coder or inter-observer reliability can be found in Cramer (1998).

Validity

The question of validity draws attention to how far a measure really measures the concept that it purports to measure. How do we know that our measure of job satisfaction is really getting at job satisfaction and not at something else? At the very minimum, a researcher who develops a new measure should establish that it has *face validity*, that is, that the measure apparently reflects the content of the concept in question.

The researcher might seek also to gauge the *concurrent validity* of the concept. Here the researcher employs a criterion on which people are known to differ and which is relevant to the concept in question. For example, some people are more often absent from work (other than through illness) than others. In order to establish the concurrent validity of our job satisfaction measure we may see how far people who are satisfied with their jobs are less likely than those who are not satisfied to be absent from work. If a lack of correspondence is found, such as frequent absentees being just as likely to be satisfied as not satisfied, we might be tempted to question whether our measure is really addressing job satisfaction. Another possible test for the validity of a new measure is *predictive validity*, whereby the researcher uses a future criterion measure, rather than a contemporaneous one as in the case of concurrent validity. With predictive validity, the researcher would take later levels of absenteeism as the criterion against which the validity of job satisfaction would be examined.

Some writers advocate that the researcher should also estimate the *construct validity* of a measure (Cronbach and Meehl, 1955). Here, the researcher is encouraged to deduce hypotheses from a theory that is relevant to the concept. For example, drawing upon ideas about the impact of technology on the experience of work (for example, Blauner, 1964), the researcher might anticipate that people who are satisfied with their jobs are less likely to work on routine jobs; those who are not satisfied are more likely to work on routine jobs. Accordingly, we could investigate this theoretical deduction by examining the relationship between job satisfaction and job routine. On the other hand, some caution is required in interpreting the absence of a relationship between job satisfaction and job routine in this example. First, the theory or the deduction that is made from it may be faulty. Second, the measure of job routine could be an invalid measure of the concept.

All the approaches to the investigation of validity that have been discussed up to now are designed to establish what Campbell and Fiske (1959) refer to as *con-*

vergent validity. In each case, the researcher is concerned to demonstrate that the measure harmonises with another measure. Campbell and Fiske argue that this process usually does not go far enough in that the researcher should really be using different measures of the same concept to see how far there is convergence. For example, in addition to devising a questionnaire-based measure of job routine, a researcher could use observers to rate the characteristics of jobs in order to distinguish between degrees of routineness in jobs in the firm (for example, Jenkins *et al.*, 1975). Convergent validity would entail demonstrating a convergence between the two measures, although it is difficult to interpret a lack of convergence since either of the two measures could be faulty. Many of the examples of convergent validation that have appeared since Campbell and Fiske's (1959) article have not involved different methods, but have employed different questionnaire research instruments (Bryman, 1989). For example, two questionnaire-based measures of job routine might be used, rather than two different methods. Campbell and Fiske went even further in suggesting that a measure should also exhibit *discriminant validity*. The investigation of discriminant validity implies that one should also search for *low* levels of correspondence between a measure and other measures which are supposed to represent other concepts. Although discriminant validity is an important facet of the validity of a measure, it is probably more important for the student to focus upon the various aspects of convergent validation that have been discussed. In order to investigate both the various types of convergent validity and discriminant validity, the various techniques covered in Chapter 8, which are concerned with relationships between pairs of variables, can be employed.

EXERCISES

1   Which of the following answers is true? A Likert scale is (a) a test for validity; (b) an approach to generating multiple-item measures; (c) a test for reliability; or (d) a method for generating dimensions of concepts?

2   When operationalising a concept, why might it be useful to consider the possibility that it comprises a number of dimensions?

3   Consider the following questions which might be used in a social survey about people's drinking habits and decide whether the variable is nominal, ordinal, interval/ratio or dichotomous:

    (a) Do you ever consume alcoholic drinks?

        Yes _____

        No _____   (go to question 5)

    (b) If you have ticked **Yes** to the previous question, which of the following alcoholic drinks do you consume most frequently? (Tick one category only.)

        Beer _____

        Spirits _____

        Wine _____

Liquors _____

Other _____

(c) How frequently do you consume alcoholic drinks? Tick the answer that comes closest to your current practice.

Daily _____

Most days _____

Once or twice week _____

Once or twice a month _____

A few times a year _____

Once or twice a year _____

(d) How many units of alcohol did you consume last week? (We can assume that the interviewer would help respondents to translate into units of alcohol.)

Number of units _____

4 In the Job Survey data, is **absence** a nominal, an ordinal, an interval/ratio, or a dichotomous variable?

5 Is test–retest reliability a test of internal or external reliability?

6 What would be the SPSS procedure for computing Cronbach's alpha for **autonom**?

7 Following on from question 6, would this be a test of internal or external reliability?

8 A researcher develops a new multiple-item measure of 'political conservatism'. He/she administers the measure to a sample of individuals and also asks them how they voted at the last general election in order to validate the new measure. The researcher relates respondents' scores to how they voted. Which of the following is the researcher assessing: (a) the measure's concurrent validity; (b) the measure's predictive validity; or (c) the measure's discriminant validity?

Chapter 5

Summarising data

When researchers are confronted with a bulk of data relating to each of a number of variables, they are faced with the task of summarising the information that has been amassed. If large amounts of data can be summarised, it becomes possible to detect patterns and tendencies that would otherwise be obscured. It is fairly easy to detect a pattern in a variable when, say, we have data on ten cases. But once we go beyond about twenty, it becomes difficult for the eye to catch patterns and trends unless the data are treated in some way. Moreover, when we want to present our collected data to an audience, it would be extremely difficult for readers to take in the relevant information. This chapter is concerned with the various procedures that may be employed to summarise a variable.

FREQUENCY DISTRIBUTIONS

Imagine that we have data on fifty-six students regarding which faculty they belong to at a university (see Table 5.1). The university has only four faculties: engineering, pure sciences, arts, and social sciences. Even though fifty-six is not a large number on which to have data, it is not particularly easy to see how students are distributed across the faculties. A first step that might be considered when summarising data relating to a nominal variable such as this (since each faculty constitutes a discrete category) is the construction of a *frequency distribution* or *frequency table*. The idea of a frequency distribution is to tell us the number of cases in each category. By 'frequency' is simply meant the number of times that something occurs. Very often we also need to compute percentages, which tell us the proportion of cases contained within each frequency, that is, *relative frequency*. In Table 5.2, the number 11 is the frequency relating to the arts category, that is, there are eleven arts students in the sample, which is 20 per cent of the total number of students.

The procedure for generating a frequency distribution with SPSS will be addressed in a later section, but in the meantime it should be realised that all that is happening in the construction of a frequency table is that the number of cases in each category is added up. Additional information in the form of the percentage

Table 5.1 The faculty membership of fifty-six students (imaginary data)

Case number	Faculty	Case number	Faculty
1	Arts	29	Eng
2	PS	30	SS
3	SS	31	PS
4	Eng	32	SS
5	Eng	33	Arts
6	SS	34	SS
7	Arts	35	Eng
8	PS	36	PS
9	Eng	37	Eng
10	SS	38	SS
11	SS	39	Arts
12	PS	40	SS
13	Eng	41	Eng
14	Arts	42	PS
15	Eng	43	SS
16	PS	44	PS
17	SS	45	Eng
18	Eng	46	Arts
19	PS	47	Eng
20	Arts	48	PS
21	Eng	49	Eng
22	Eng	50	Arts
23	PS	51	SS
24	Arts	52	Eng
25	Eng	53	Arts
26	PS	54	Eng
27	Arts	55	SS
28	PS	56	SS

Note: Eng = Engineering; PS = Pure Sciences; SS = Social Sciences

that the number of cases in each category constitutes is usually provided. This provides information about the relative frequency of the occurrence of each category of a variable. It gives a good indication of the relative preponderance of each category in the sample. Table 5.2 provides the frequency table for the data in Table 5.1. Percentages have been rounded up or down to a whole number (using the simple rule that 0.5 and above is rounded up and below 0.5 is rounded down) to make the table easier to read. The letter n is often employed to refer to the number of cases in each category (that is, the frequency). An alternative way of presenting a frequency table for the data summarised in Table 5.2 is to omit the frequencies for each category and to present only the relative percentages. This approach reduces the amount of information that the reader must absorb. When this option is taken, it is necessary to provide the total number of cases (that is, $n=56$) beneath the column of percentages.

Table 5.2 Frequency table for faculty
              membership

Faculty	n	Per cent
Engineering	18	32
Pure Sciences	13	23
Arts	11	20
Social Sciences	14	25
Total	56	100

Table 5.2 can readily be adapted to provide a diagrammatic version of the data. Such diagrams are usually called *bar charts* or *bar diagrams* and are often preferred to tables because they are more easily assimilated. A bar chart presents a column for the number or percentage of cases relating to each category. Figure 5.1 presents a bar chart for the data in Table 5.1 in terms of the number of cases. On the horizontal axis the name of each category is presented. There is no need to order them in any way (for example, short to long bars). The bars should not touch each other but should be kept clearly separate. It should be realised that the bar chart does not provide more information than Table 5.2; indeed, some information is lost – the percentages. Its main advantage is the ease with which it can be interpreted, a characteristic that may be especially useful when data are being presented to people who may be unfamiliar with statistical material.

When a variable is at the interval/ratio level, the data will have to be grouped in order to be presented in a frequency table. The number of cases in each grouping must then be calculated. As an example, the Job Survey data on **income** may be examined. We have data on sixty-eight individuals (two are missing), but if the data are not grouped there are thirty-three categories, which is far too many for a frequency table. Moreover, the frequencies in each category would be far too small. In Table 5.3, a frequency table is presented of the data on **income**. Six categories are employed. In constructing categories such as these a number of points should be borne in mind. First, it is sometimes suggested that the number of

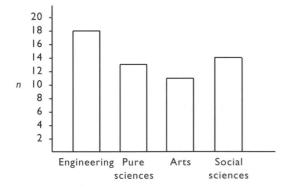

Figure 5.1 Bar chart of data on number of students per faculty

Table 5.3 Frequency table for **income**
(Job Survey data)

£	n	Per cent
Below 12,000	1	1.5
12,000–13,999	16	23.5
14,000–15,999	20	29.4
16,000–17,999	22	32.4
18,000–19,999	7	10.3
20,000 and over	2	2.9
Total	68	100.0

categories should be between six and twenty, since too few or too many categories can distort the shape of the distribution of the underlying variable (see, for example, Bohrnstedt and Knoke, 1982). However, it is not necessarily the case that the number of categories will affect the shape of the distribution. Also, when there are relatively few cases the number of categories will have to fall below six in order for there to be a reasonable number of cases in each category. On the other hand, a large number of categories will not be easy for the reader to assimilate, and in this regard Bohrnstedt and Knoke's rule of thumb that the upper limit should be twenty categories seems slightly high. Second, the categories must be discrete. You should never group so that you have categories such as: 12,000 or less;

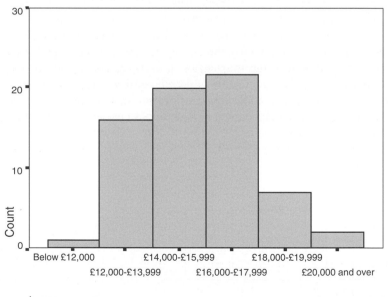

income groups

Figure 5.2 Histogram for **income** data (Job Survey data)

12,000–14000; 14,000–16,000; and so on. Which categories would incomes of £12,000 and £14,000 belong to? Categories must be discrete, as in Table 5.3, so that there can be no uncertainty about which one a case should be allocated to. Note that in Table 5.3, the reader's attention is drawn to the fact that there are two missing cases. The presence of two missing cases raises the question of whether percentages should be calculated in terms of all seventy cases in the Job Survey sample or the sixty-eight on whom we have income data. Most writers prefer the latter since the inclusion of all cases in the base for the calculation of the percentage can result in misleading interpretations, especially when there might be a large number of missing cases in connection with a particular variable.

The information in Table 5.3 can be usefully presented diagrammatically as a *histogram*. A histogram is similar to a bar chart, except that the bars are in contact with each other to reflect the continuous nature of the categories of the variable in question. Figure 5.2 presents a histogram produced by SPSS for the **income** data. Its advantages are the same as those of the bar chart.

If an ordinal variable is being analysed, grouping of categories is rarely necessary. In the case of the Job Survey data, a variable such as **skill**, which can assume only four categories, will not need to be grouped. The number of cases in each of the four categories can simply be added up and the percentages computed. A histogram can be used to display such data since the categories of the variable are ordered.

Using SPSS to produce frequency tables and histograms

In order to generate a frequency table for **income**, we need to group the data; otherwise we shall get a frequency count and percentage for every single income in the sample. We would have separate bars for each income within the sample. In a large sample, that could represent a lot of bars. To group the data, we need to use the **Recode** procedure. In doing this, we shall be creating a new variable which will be called **incomegp** (that is, **income group**s). The aim is to group people into six income groups: below £12,000; £12,000–13,999; £14,000–15,999; £16,000–17,999; £18,000–19,999; and £20,000 and above. The following sequence will accomplish this:

→**Transform** →**Recode** →**Into Different Variables...** [opens **Recode into Different Variables** dialog box shown in Box 5.1]
→**income** →▶button [puts **income** in **Numeric Variable->Output Variable:** box] →box beneath **Output Variable Name:** and type **incomegp** →**Change** [puts **incomegp** in **Numeric Variable->Output Variable:** box] →**Old and New Values...** [opens **Recode into Different Variables: Old and New Values** subdialog box shown in Box 5.2]
→circle by **System- or user-missing** and in the box to the right of **Value** type **0** [this specifies that 0 will be recognised as a missing value] →circle by **Range:**

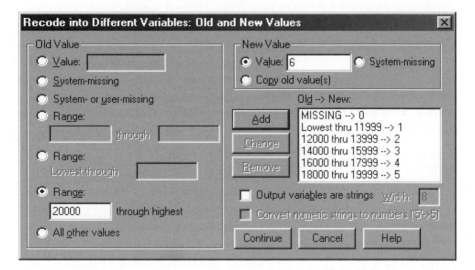

Box 5.1 Recoding **income** into **incomegp**

Box 5.2 **Recode into Different Variables: Old and New Values** subdialog
box

Lowest through and type **11999** in box after **through** ➔box by **Value:** below
New Value and type **1** ➔**Add** [the new value will appear in the **Old —> New:**
box] ➔circle by **Range:** and in box below type **12000** and in box after **through**
type **13999** ➔box by **Value** below **New Value** and type **2** ➔ first box below
Range: and type **14000** and in box after **through** type **15999** ➔box by **Value**
below **New Value** and type **3** ➔box below **Range:** and type **16000** and in box
after **through** type **17999** ➔box by **Value** below **New Value** and type **4** ➔box
below **Range:** and type **18000** and in box after **through** type **19999** ➔box by

Box 5.3 **Frequencies** dialog box

Table 5.4 Frequency table for **incomegp** (SPSS output)

income groups

		Frequency	Percent	Valid Percent	Cumulative Percent
Valid	Below £12,000	1	1.4	1.5	1.5
	£12,000-£13,999	16	22.9	23.5	25.0
	£14,000-£15,999	20	28.6	29.4	54.4
	£16,000-£17,999	22	31.4	32.4	86.8
	£18,000-£19,999	7	10.0	10.3	97.1
	£20,000 and over	2	2.9	2.9	100.0
	Total	68	97.1	100.0	
Missing	.00	2	2.9		
Total		70	100.0		

Va̱lue below **New Value** and type **5** →circle by **Range: through highest** and type **20000** in box →box by **Va̱lue** below **New Value** and type **6** →**A̱dd** →**Continue** [closes **Recode into Different Variables: Old and New Values** subdialog box]
→**OK**

It would then be necessary to define the **value labels** for the six categories of **incomegp** (see Chapter 2 for a description of how this is done).

The following sequence will generate the frequency table output in Table 5.4:

→**A̱nalyze** →**De̱scriptive Statistics** →**F̱requencies...** [opens **Frequencies** dialog box shown in Box 5.3]

→**income groups [incomegp]** →▶button [puts **incomegp** in <u>V</u>**ariable[s]:** box]
→**OK**

Table 5.4 provides the number of people in each category (**Frequency**) and three percentages: the frequency associated with each category as a percentage of all cases (**Percent**); the frequency associated with each category as a percentage of all cases on which data exist and which therefore excludes the two cases for whom data are missing (**Valid Percent**); and the cumulative percentage (**Cum Percent**).

For a histogram of **income**, the following sequence should be followed:

→<u>G</u>**raphs** →**Hi<u>s</u>togram...** [opens **Histogram** dialog box]
→**income** →▶button [puts **income** in <u>V</u>**ariable:** box] →**OK**

The resulting histogram will employ income bands defined by the SPSS default criteria.

To produce a bar chart for a nominal variable like **ethnicgp**, the following sequence can be followed:

→<u>G</u>**raphs** →<u>B</u>**ar...** [opens **Bar Charts** dialog box shown in Box 5.4]
→**Simple** →**Summaries for groups of <u>c</u>ases** →**Define** [opens **Define Simple Bar: Summaries for Groups of Cases** subdialog box shown in Box 5.5]
→**ethnicgp** →▶button by **Category Axis** [puts **ethnicgp** in box] →<u>N</u> **of cases** beneath **Bars Represent** [if this has not already been selected, otherwise continue without doing this] →**OK**

Box 5.4 **Bar Charts** dialog box

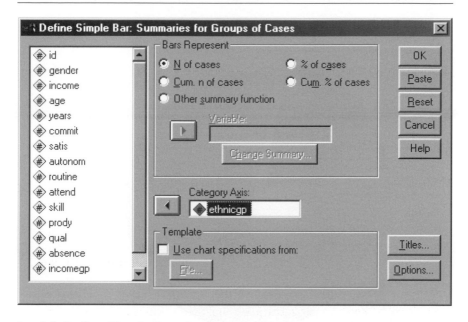

Box 5.5 **Define Simple Bar: Summaries for Groups of Cases** subdialog box

An alternative way of presenting data relating to a nominal variable is a *pie chart*, which displays the number of cases in each category in terms of slices of a circle. This can be a useful means of presenting data when the object is to emphasise the relative size of each slice in relation to the sample as a whole. Figure 5.3 presents a basic pie chart for **ethnicgp** generated by SPSS. Initially, the following sequence should be followed:

➔**Graphs** ➔**Pie...** [opens **Pie Charts** dialog box shown in Box 5.6]
➔**Summaries for groups of cases** ➔**Define** [opens **Define Pie: Summaries for Groups of Cases** subdialog shown in Box 5.7]
➔**ethnicgp** ➔▶button by **Define Slices by** [puts **ethnicgp** in the box] ➔**N of cases** beneath **Slices Represent:** [if this has *not* already been selected, otherwise continue without doing this] ➔**OK**

A pie chart will be produced with each slice in a different colour. If you are not able to print this out with a colour printer, you will need to edit the chart so that each slice is distinguishable. The chart in Figure 5.3 was drawn using two separate steps: white was applied to all the slices and separate patterns were applied to each slice. The following steps will achieve this:

Double click anywhere in the chart. This will bring up the **Chart Editor**. The chart will appear in the **Chart Editor** and the main figure will appear shaded.

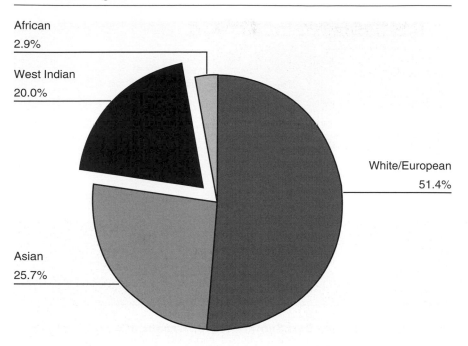

Figure 5.3 Pie chart for **ethnicgp** (Job Survey data)

To fill each slice with white:

➔any slice in the chart, which will result in dots appearing around the edge ➔**F<u>o</u>rmat** ➔**<u>C</u>olor...** [a palette of colours will appear] ➔**<u>F</u>ill** ➔white ➔**Apply** ➔another slice and apply to this and all the other slices, though it may be useful to have one slice in a very dark colour ➔**Close**

To create a different pattern for each slice:

➔any slice in the chart, which will result in dots appearing around the edge ➔**F<u>o</u>rmat** ➔**<u>F</u>ill pattern...** [a palette of patterns will appear and you should decide which ones you want] ➔chosen pattern ➔**Apply** ➔another slice ➔another pattern [remember that you are applying a *different* pattern to each slice] ➔**Apply** [and continue until each white slice has a different pattern] ➔**Close**

Note that you will need previously to assign **value labels** to produce the labels found in Figure 5.3. The percentage of the sample that each slice represents can be added (as in Figure 5.3) when in the **Chart Editor** by ➔**<u>C</u>hart** and then ➔**<u>O</u>ptions...** and then placing a tick **<u>P</u>ercents** [there should also be a tick by **<u>T</u>ext**].

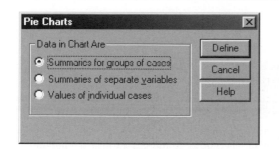

Box 5.6 **Pie Charts** dialog box

Define Pie: Summaries for Groups of Cases

Slices Represent
- N of cases
- % of cases
- Cum. n of cases
- Cum. % of cases
- Other summary function

Variable:

Change Summary...

Define Slices by:
ethnicgp

Template
Use chart specifications from:
File...

OK
Paste
Reset
Cancel
Help

Titles...
Options...

Box 5.7 **Define Pie: Summaries for Groups of Cases** subdialog box

You can also create an 'exploded' pie effect (as in Figure 5.3), whereby one slice becomes detached from the pie so that it can be emphasised. To do this:

→Format →Exploded Slice

Similar changes can be made to all SPSS figures (for example, bar charts) by double clicking on the chart in question and bringing up the **Chart Editor**. This allows you to change colours, introduce patterns, assign figure captions, and provide various items of additional information.

MEASURING CENTRAL TENDENCY

One of the most important ways of summarising a distribution of values for a variable is to establish its *central tendency* – the typical value in a distribution. Where, for example, do values in a distribution tend to concentrate? To many readers this may mean trying to find the 'average' of a distribution of values. However, statisticians mean a number of different measures when they talk about averages. Three measures of average (that is, central tendency) are usually discussed in textbooks: the arithmetic mean, the median and the mode. Stephen J. Gould, a palaeontologist who is well known for his popular writings on science, illustrates the first two of these measures of average when he writes:

> A politician in power might say with pride, 'The mean income of our citizens is $15,000 per year.' The leader of the opposition might retort, 'But half our citizens make less than $10,000 per year.' Both are right, but neither cites a statistic with impassive objectivity. The first invokes a mean, the second a median.
>
> (Gould, 1991: 473)

While this comment does little to reassure us about the possible misuse of statistics, it does illustrate well the different ways in which average can be construed.

The arithmetic mean

The arithmetic mean is a method for measuring the average of a distribution which conforms to most people's notion of what an average is. Consider the following distribution of values:

12   10   7   9   8   15   2   19   7   10   8   16

The arithmetic mean consists of adding up all the values (that is, 123) and dividing by the number of values (that is, 12), which results in an arithmetic mean of 10.25. It is this kind of calculation which leads to such seemingly bizarre statements as 'the average number of children is 2.37'. However, the arithmetic mean, which is often symbolised as x, is by far the most commonly used method of gauging central tendency. Many of the statistical tests encountered later in this book are directly concerned with comparing means deriving from different samples or groups of cases (for example, analysis of variance – see Chapter 7). The arithmetic mean is easy to understand and to interpret, which heightens its appeal. Its chief limitation is that it is vulnerable to extreme values, in that it may be unduly affected by very high or very low values which can respectively increase or decrease its magnitude. This is particularly likely to occur when there are relatively few values; when there are many values, it would take a very extreme value to distort the arithmetic mean. For example, if the number 59 is substituted for 19 in the previous distribution of twelve values, the mean would be 13.58, rather than 10.25,

which constitutes a substantial difference and could be taken to be a poor representation of the distribution as a whole. Similarly, in Table 8.10 in Chapter 8, the
variable 'size of firm' contains an outlier (case number 20) which is a firm of 2,700
employees whereas the next largest has 640 employees. The mean for this variable
is 499, but if we exclude the outlier it is 382.6. Again, we see that an outlier can
have a very large impact on the arithmetic mean, especially when the number of
cases in the sample is quite small.

The median

The median is the mid-point in a distribution of values. It splits a distribution of
values in half. Imagine that the values in a distribution are arrayed from low to
high, for example, 2, 4, 7, 9, 10, the median is the middle value, that is, 7. When
there is an even number of values, the average of the two middle values is taken.
Thus, in the former group of twelve values, to calculate the mean we need to array
them as follows

$$2 \quad 7 \quad 7 \quad 8 \quad 8 \quad \underline{9 \quad 10} \quad 10 \quad 12 \quad 15 \quad 16 \quad 19.$$

Thus in this array of twelve values, we take the two underlined values – the sixth
and seventh – and divide their sum by 2, that is, $(9+10)/2=9.5$. This is slightly
lower than the arithmetic mean of 10.25, which is almost certainly due to the presence of three fairly large values at the upper end – 15, 16, 19. If we had the value
59 instead of 19, although we know that the mean would be higher at 13.58 the
median would be unaffected, because it emphasises the middle of the distribution
and ignores the ends. For this reason, many writers suggest that when there is an
outlying value which may distort the mean, the median should be considered
because it will engender a more representative indication of the central tendency of
a group of values. On the other hand, the median is less intuitively easy to understand and not all the values in a distribution are used to calculate it. Moreover,
the mean's vulnerability to distortion as a consequence of extreme values is less
pronounced when there are a large number of cases.

The mode

This final indicator of central tendency is rarely used in research reports, but is
often mentioned in textbooks. The mode is simply the value that occurs most
frequently in a distribution. In the foregoing array of twelve values, there are three
modes – 7, 8 and 10. Unlike the mean, which strictly speaking should only be used
in relation to interval variables, the mode can be employed at any measurement
level. The median can be employed in relation to interval and ordinal, but not
nominal, variables. Thus, although the mode appears more flexible, it is infre-
quently used, in part because it does not use all the values of a distribution and is
not easy to interpret when there is a number of modes.

MEASURING DISPERSION

In addition to being interested in the typical or representative score for a distribution of values, researchers are usually interested in the amount of variation shown by that distribution. This is what is meant by *dispersion*: how widely spread a distribution is. Dispersion can provide us with important information. For example, we may find two roughly comparable firms in which the mean income of manual workers is identical. However, in one firm the salaries of these workers are more widely spread, with both considerably lower and higher salaries than in the other firm. Thus, although the mean income is the same, one firm exhibits much greater dispersion in incomes than the other. This is important information that can usefully be employed to add to measures of central tendency.

The most obvious measure of dispersion is to take the highest and lowest value in a distribution and to subtract the latter from the former. This is known as the *range*. While easy to understand, it suffers from the disadvantage of being susceptible to distortion from extreme values. This point can be illustrated by the imaginary data in Table 5.5, which shows the marks out of a hundred achieved in a mathematics test by two classes of twenty students, each of which was taught by a different teacher. The two classes exhibit similar means, but the patterns of the two distributions of values are highly dissimilar. Teacher A's class has a fairly bunched

Table 5.5 Results of a test of mathematical ability for the students of two teachers (imaginary data)

	Teacher A	Teacher B
	65	57
	70	49
	66	46
	59	79
	57	72
	62	54
	66	66
	71	65
	58	63
	67	76
	61	45
	68	95
	63	62
	65	68
	71	50
	69	53
	67	58
	74	65
	72	69
	60	72
Arithmetic mean	65.55	63.2
Standard deviation	4.91	12.37
Median	66	64

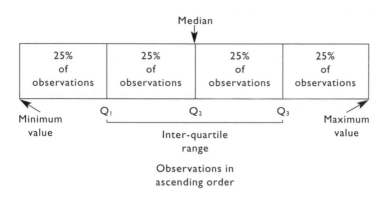

Figure 5.4 The inter-quartile range

distribution, whereas that of Teacher B's class is much more dispersed: whereas the lowest mark attained in Teacher A's class is 57, the lowest for Teacher B is 45. Indeed, there are eight marks in Teacher B's class that are below 57. However, whereas the highest mark in Teacher A's class is 74, three of Teacher B's class exceed this figure – one with a very high 95. Although the latter distribution is more dispersed, the calculation of the range seems to exaggerate its dispersion. The range for Teacher A is 74–57, that is, a range of 17. For teacher B, the range is 95–45, that is, 50. This exaggerates the amount of dispersion since all but three of the values are between 72 and 45, implying a range of 27 for the majority of the values.

One solution to this problem is to eliminate the extreme values. The *inter-quartile range*, for example, is sometimes recommended in this connection (see Figure 5.4). This entails arraying a range of values in ascending order. The array is divided into four equal portions, so that the lowest 25 per cent are in the first portion and the highest 25 per cent are in the last portion. These portions are used to generate quartiles. Take the earlier array from which the median was calculated:

2   7   7   8   8   9   10   10   12   15   16   19
        ⇧   ⇧
       1st   3rd
     quartile   quartile

The first quartile (Q1), often called the 'lower quartile', will be between 7 and 8. SPSS calculates it as 7.25. The third quartile (Q3), often called the 'upper quartile', is 14.25. Therefore the inter-quartile range is the difference between the third and first quartiles, that is, 14.25−7.25=7. As Figure 5.4 indicates, the median is the second quartile, but is not a component of the calculation of the inter-quartile range. The main advantage of this measure of dispersion is that it eliminates extreme values, but its chief limitation is that in ignoring 50 per cent of the values in a distribution it loses a lot of information. A compromise is the *decile range*, which divides a distribution into ten portions (deciles) and, in a similar manner to the inter-quartile range, eliminates the highest and lowest portions. In this case, only 20 per cent of the distribution is lost.

By far the most commonly used method of summarising dispersion is the *standard deviation*. In essence, the standard deviation calculates the average amount of deviation from the mean. Its calculation is somewhat more complicated than this definition implies. A further description of the standard deviation can be found in Chapter 7. The standard deviation reflects the degree to which the values in a distribution differ from the arithmetic mean. The standard deviation is usually presented in tandem with the mean, since it is difficult to determine its meaning in the absence of the mean.

We can compare the two distributions in Table 5.5. Although the means are very similar, the standard deviation for Teacher B's class (12.37) is much larger than that for Teacher A (4.91). Thus, the standard deviation permits the direct comparison of degrees of dispersal for comparable samples and measures. A further advantage is that it employs all the values in a distribution. It summarises in a single value the amount of dispersion in a distribution, which, when used in conjunction with the mean, is easy to interpret. The standard deviation can be affected by extreme values, but since its calculation is affected by the number of cases, the distortion is less pronounced than with the range. On the other hand, the possibility of distortion from extreme values must be borne in mind. None the less, unless there are very good reasons for not wanting to use the standard deviation, it should be used whenever a measure of dispersion is required. It is routinely reported in research reports and widely recognised as the main measure of dispersion.

This consideration of dispersion has tended to emphasise interval variables. The standard deviation can only be employed in relation to such variables. The range and inter-quartile range can be used in relation to ordinal variables, but this does not normally happen, while tests for dispersion in nominal variables would be

Box 5.8 **Explore** dialog box

inappropriate. Probably the best ways of examining dispersion for nominal and ordinal variables is through bar charts, histograms and frequency tables.

Measuring Central Tendency and Dispersion with SPSS

All these statistics can be generated in SPSS. Taking **income** as an illustration, the following sequence should be followed:

→**Analyze** →**Descriptive Statistics** →**Explore...** [opens **Explore** dialog box shown in Box 5.8]

→**income** →▶button by **Dependent List:** [puts **income** in **Dependent List:** box] →**OK**

The resulting output is in Table 5.6. The following items that have been covered

Table 5.6 **Explore** output for **income**

Descriptives

			Statistic	Std. Error
INCOME	Mean		15638.24	242.04
	95% Confidence Interval for Mean	Lower Bound	15155.13	
		Upper Bound	16121.34	
	5% Trimmed Mean		15582.35	
	Median		15600.00	
	Variance		3983591	
	Std. Deviation		1995.89	
	Minimum		11800	
	Maximum		21000	
	Range		9200	
	Interquartile Range		3500.00	
	Skewness		.370	.291
	Kurtosis		-.294	.574

```
INCOME Stem-and-Leaf Plot

 Frequency    Stem &  Leaf

     1.00       11 .  8
     3.00       12 .  448
    13.00       13 .  0244466668888
    10.00       14 .  0022246668
    10.00       15 .  0000246688
    11.00       16 .  00002446666
    11.00       17 .  00244666688
     6.00       18 .  000226
     1.00       19 .  0
     1.00       20 .  6
     1.00       21 .  0

 Stem width:    1000
 Each leaf:       1 case(s)
```

above will be produced: arithmetic mean (**Mean**), median, range, minimum and maximum values, standard deviation (**Std Deviation**), and the inter-quartile range.

STEMS AND LEAVES, BOXES AND WHISKERS

In 1977, John Tukey published a highly influential book entitled *Exploratory Data Analysis*, which sought to introduce readers to a variety of techniques he had developed that emphasise simple arithmetic computation and diagrammatic displays of data. Although the approach he advocates is antithetical to many of the techniques conventionally employed by data analysts, including the bulk of techniques examined in this book, some of Tukey's displays can be usefully appended to more orthodox procedures. Two diagrammatic presentations of data are very relevant to the present discussion: the *stem and leaf display* and the *boxplot* (sometimes called the *box and whisker plot*).

The stem and leaf display

The stem and leaf display is an extremely simple means of presenting data on an interval variable in a manner similar to a histogram, but without the loss of information that a histogram necessarily entails. It can be easily constructed by hand, although this would be more difficult with very large amounts of data. In order to illustrate the stem and leaf display, data on one indicator of local authority performance are taken. For a number of years, the British government has given the Audit Commission the task of collecting data on the performance of local authorities, so that their performance can be compared. One of the criteria of performance relates to the percentage of special needs reports issued within six months. A good deal of variation could be discerned with respect to this criterion, as the author of an article in *The Times* noted:

> If a child in Sunderland needs a report drawn up on its special educational needs, it has no chance of receiving this within six months. If the child moved a mile or two down the road into Durham, there would be an 80 per cent chance that the report would be issued in that time.

(Murray, 1995: 32)

Whether such data really measure efficiency is, of course, a matter of whether the measure is *valid* (see Chapter 4), but there is no doubt that there is a great deal of variation with respect to the percentage of reports issued within six months. As Table 5.7 shows, the percentage varies between 0 and 95 per cent.

Figure 5.5 provides a stem and leaf display for this variable which we call 'needs'. The display has two main components. First, the digits in the middle column make up the stem. These constitute the starting parts for presenting each value in a distribution. Each of the digits that form the stem represents age in tens, that is, 0 refers to single digit numbers; 1 to tens; 2 to twenties; 3 to thirties; and so

Table 5.7 Percentage of special needs reports issued within six months in local authorities in England and Wales, 1993–4

London boroughs		English counties		Metropolitan authorities		Welsh counties	
Inner London		Avon	11	**Greater**		Clwyd	30
City of London	*	Bedfordshire	25	**Manchester**		Dyfed	67
Camden	48	Berkshire	16	Bolton	9	Gwent	17
Greenwich	14	Buckinghamshire	69	Bury	16	Gwynedd	88
Hackney	36	Cambridgeshire	7	Manchester	35	Mid	
Ham & Fulham	6	Cheshire	25	Oldham	50	Glamorgan	48
Islington	44	Cleveland	32	Rochdale	0	Powys	80
Ken & Chelsea	8	Cornwall	3	Salford	10	South	
Lambeth	4	Cumbria	35	Stockport	16	Glamorgan	45
Lewisham	12	Derbyshire	17	Tameside	16	West	
Southwark	10	Devon	55	Trafford	11	Glamorgan	4
Tower Hamlets	37	Dorset	33	Wigan	21		
Wandsworth	4	Durham	72	**Merseyside**			
Westminster	63	East Sussex	8	Knowsley	8		
Outer London		Essex	29	Liverpool	95		
Barking &		Gloucestershire	45	St Helens	21		
Dagenham	22	Hampshire	12	Sefton	37		
Barnet	40	Hereford &Worcs	3	Wirral	13		
Bexley	37	Hertfordshire	61	**SouthYorkshire**			
Brent	23	Humberside	14	Barnsley	15		
Bromley	24	Isle of Wight	60	Doncaster	1		
Croydon	27	Kent	15	Rotherham	10		
Ealing	3	Lancashire	14	Sheffield	4		
Enfield	2	Leicestershire	*	**Tyne & Wear**			
Haringey	10	Lincolnshire	36	Gateshead	4		
Harrow	1	Norfolk	1	Newcastle upon			
Havering	0	Northamptonshire	48	Tyne	30		
Hillingdon	7	Northumberland	79	North Tyneside	48		
Hounslow	20	North Yorkshire	34	South Tyneside	5		
Kingston upon		Nottinghamshire	10	Sunderland	0		
Thames	27	Oxfordshire	22	**West Midlands**			
Merton	16	Shropshire	15	Birmingham	5		
Newham	3	Somerset	50	Coventry	20		
Redbridge	34	Staffordshire	20	Dudley	41		
Richmond		Suffolk	27	Sandwell	1		
upon Thames	27	Surrey	55	Solihull	31		
Sutton	6	Warwickshire	26	Walsall	3		
Waltham Forest	24	West Sussex	14	Wolverhampton	3		
		Wiltshire	30	**West Yorkshire**			
				Bradford	25		
				Calderdale	2		
				Kirklees.	38		
				Leeds	17		
				Wakefield	15		

Note: * = missing or doubtful information.
Source: adapted from *The Times*, 30 March 1995: 32

```
NEEDS Stem-and-Leaf Plot

Frequency      Stem &  Leaf
    20.00         0 .  00011112233333344444
    10.00         0 .  5566778889
    14.00         1 .  00000112234444
    12.00         1 .  555566666777
    10.00         2 .  0001122344
     9.00         2 .  555677779
     8.00         3 .  00012344
     8.00         3 .  55667778
     3.00         4 .  014
     6.00         4 .  558888
     2.00         5 .  00
     2.00         5 .  55
     3.00         6 .  013
     2.00         6 .  79
     1.00         7 .  2
     4.00 Extremes    (>=79)

Stem width:      10.00
Each leaf:        1 case(s)
```

Figure 5.5 Stem and leaf display for **needs**

on. To the right of the stem are the leaves, each of which represents an item of data which is linked to the stem. Thus, the 0 to the right of the 0 refers to the lowest value in the distribution, namely the percentage figure of 0. We can see that three authorities failed to issue any reports within six months and four issued only 1 per cent of reports within six months. When we come to the row starting with 1, we can see that five managed to issue 10 per cent of reports within six months. It is important to ensure that all the leaves – the digits to the right of the stem – are vertically aligned. It is not necessary for the leaves to be ordered in magnitude, that is, from 0 to 9, but it is easier to read. We can see that the distribution is very bunched in the middle of the distribution. The appearance of the diagram has been controlled by requesting that incremental jumps are in tens, that is, first tens, then twenties, then thirties, and so on. The output can also be controlled by requesting that any outliers are separately positioned. Practitioners of exploratory data analysis use a specific criterion for the identification of outliers. Outliers at the low end of the range will be below:

first quartile – (1.5 × the inter-quartile range)

and at the high end of the range will be above:

third quartile – (1.5 × the inter-quartile range).

The first quartile for 'needs' is 8.0 and the third quartile is 36.0. Substituting in these two simple equations means that outliers will need to be below −36.0 or above 78.0. Using this criterion, four outliers (**Extremes**) are identified (see Figure 5.5). To produce a stem and leaf display, we follow almost exactly the same procedure as we did for producing measures of central tendency and dispersion (see Box 5.5):

→**Analyze** →**Descriptive Statistics** →**Explore...** [opens **Explore** dialog box shown in Box 5.8]
→**needs** →▶button by **Dependent List:** [puts **needs** in **Dependent List:** box]
→**Plots** in box by **Display** →**OK**

The output is in Figure 5.5. The figures in the column to the left of the starting parts represent the frequency for each. We can also see that there are missing data for two authorities.

The stem and leaf display provides a similar presentation to a histogram, in that it gives a sense of the shape of the distribution (such as whether values tend to be bunched at one end), the degree of dispersion and whether there are outlying values. However, unlike the histogram it retains all the information, so that values can be directly examined to see whether particular ones tend to predominate.

The boxplot

Figure 5.6 provides the skeletal outline of a basic boxplot. The box comprises the middle 50 per cent of observations. Thus the lower end of the box, in terms of the measure to which it refers, is the first quartile and the upper end is the third

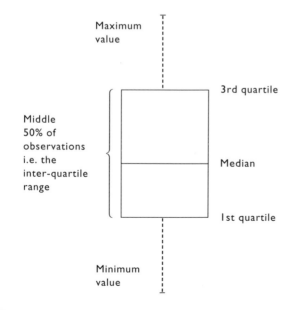

Figure 5.6 Boxplot

quartile. In other words, the box comprises the inter-quartile range. The line in the box is the median. The broken lines (the whiskers) extend downwards to the lowest value in the distribution and upwards to the largest value *excluding outliers*, that is, extreme values, which are separately indicated. It has a number of advantages. Like the stem and leaf display, the boxplot provides information about the shape and dispersion of a distribution. For example, is the box closer to one end or is it near the middle? The former would denote that values tend to bunch at one end. In this case, the bulk of the observations are at the lower end of the distribution, as is the median. This provides further information about the shape of the distribution, since it raises the question of whether the median is closer to one end of the box, as it is in this case. On the other hand, the boxplot does not retain information like the stem and leaf display. Figure 5.7 provides a boxplot of the data from Table 5.6. The four outliers are signalled, using the previously discussed criterion. It is clear that in half the authorities (all those below the line representing the median) 20 per cent or fewer reports are issued within six months.

When a stem and leaf display is requested as above, a boxplot will also be produced and will appear in the SPSS Output Viewer. In other words, following the sequence stipulated on page 89 will generate both a stem and leaf display *and* a boxplot.

Both of these exploratory data analysis techniques can be recommended as providing useful first steps in gaining a feel for data when you first start to analyse

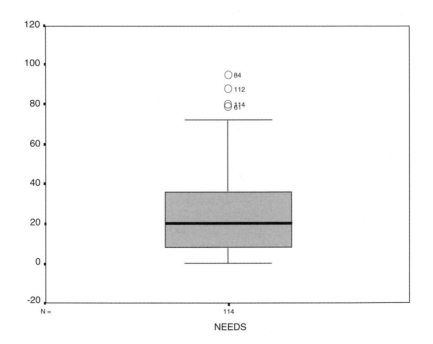

Figure 5.7 Boxplot for **needs** (SPSS output)

them. Should they be used as alternatives to histograms and other more common diagrammatic approaches? Here they suffer from the disadvantage of not being well known. The stem and leaf diagram is probably the easier of the two to assimilate, since the boxplot diagram requires an understanding of quartiles and the median. If used in relation to audiences who are likely to be unfamiliar with these techniques, they may generate some discomfort even if a full explanation is provided. On the other hand, for audiences who are (or should be) familiar with these ideas, they have much to recommend them.

THE SHAPE OF A DISTRIBUTION

On a number of occasions, reference has been made to the shape of a distribution. For example, values in a distribution may tend to cluster at one end of the distribution or in the middle. In this section, we shall be more specific about the idea of shape and introduce some ideas that are central to some aspects of data analysis that will be encountered in later chapters.

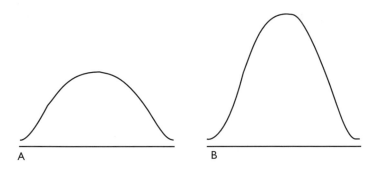

A   B

Figure 5.8 Two normal distributions

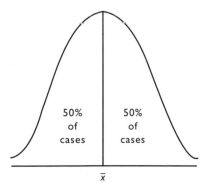

Figure 5.9 The normal distribution and the mean

Statisticians recognise a host of different possible distribution curves. By far the most important is the *normal distribution*. The normal distribution is a bell-shaped curve. It can take a number of different forms depending upon the degree to which the data are dispersed. Two examples of normal distribution curves are presented in Figure 5.8. The term 'normal' is potentially very misleading, because perfectly normal distributions are very rarely found in reality. However, the values of a variable may approximate to a normal distribution and, when they do, we tend to think of them as having the properties of a normal distribution. Many of the most common statistical techniques used by social scientists presume that the variables being analysed are nearly normally distributed (see the discussion of parametric and non-parametric tests in Chapter 7).

The normal distribution should be thought of as subsuming all the cases which it describes beneath its curve: 50 per cent will lie on one side of the arithmetic mean; the other 50 per cent on the other side (see Figure 5.9). The median value will be identical to the mean. As the curve implies, most values will be close to the mean. This is why the curve peaks at the mean. But the tapering off at either side indicates that as we move in either direction away from the mean, fewer and fewer cases are found. Only a small proportion will be found at its outer reaches. People's heights illustrate this fairly well. The mean height for an adult woman in the UK is 5 ft 3 ins (160.9 cm). If women's heights are normally distributed, we would expect that most women would cluster around this mean. Very few will be

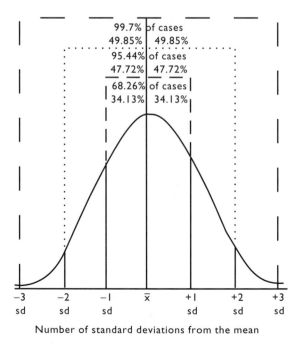

Figure 5.10 Properties of the normal distribution

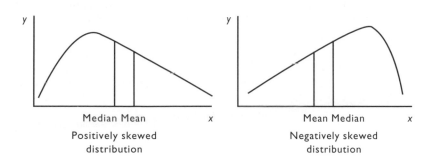

Figure 5.11 Positively and negatively skewed distributions

very short or very tall. We know that women's heights have these properties, though whether they are perfectly normally distributed is another matter.

The normal distribution displays some interesting properties that have been determined by statisticians. These properties are illustrated in Figure 5.10. In a perfectly normal distribution:

68.26 per cent of cases will be within one standard deviation of the mean;
95.44 per cent of cases will be within two standard deviations of the mean;
99.7 per cent of cases will be within three standard deviations of the mean.

These features of a normal distribution become very significant when we explore the ways in which social scientists seek to infer features of populations from samples, which is the focus of Chapter 6.

It is important to realise that some variables will not follow the shape of the normal distribution curve. In some cases, they may depart very strikingly from it. This tendency is most clearly evident when the values in a distribution are *skewed* – that is, they tend to cluster at either end. When this occurs, the mean and median no longer coincide. These ideas are illustrated in Figure 5.11. The left-hand diagram shows a curve that is *positively skewed* in that cases tend to cluster to the left and there is a long 'tail' to the right. The variable 'needs' is an illustration of a positively skewed distribution, as the boxplot in Figure 5.7 suggests (the mean is 24.75 and the median is 20.00). In the right-hand diagram, the curve is *negatively skewed*. Another kind of distribution is one which possesses more than one peak.

Although there is a recognition that some variables in the social sciences do not exhibit the characteristics of a normal curve and that therefore we often have to treat variables as though they were normally distributed, when there is a very marked discrepancy from a normal distribution, such as in the two cases in Figure 5.10, some caution is required. For example, many writers would argue that it would not be appropriate to apply certain kinds of statistical test to variables which are profoundly skewed when that test presumes normally distributed data. Very often, skewness or other pronounced departures from a normal distribution can be established from the examination of a frequency table or of a histogram. SPSS

Box 5.9 **Frequencies: Statistics** subdialog box

provides a measure of skewness, which can be generated through the following sequence (using **income** as an illustration):

→**Analyze** →**Descriptive Statistics** →**Frequencies...** [opens **Frequencies** dialog box shown in Box 5.3]
→**income** →▶button →**Statistics** [opens **Frequencies: Statistics** subdialog box shown in Box 5.9]
→**Skewness** below **Distribution** →**Continue** [closes **Frequencies: Statistics** subdialog box]
→**OK**

If there is no skew, or in other words if the variable is normally distributed, a value of zero or nearly zero will be registered. If there is a negative value, the data are negatively skewed; if the value is positive, the data are positively skewed. On the other hand, this test is not easy to interpret and there is much to be said for a visual interpretation of the data to discern excessive skew. This can be done through a frequency table, or through a diagrammatic presentation, such as a histogram or a stem and leaf display.

EXERCISES

1   What is the appropriate SPSS procedure for producing a frequency table for **prody** (Job Survey data), along with percentages and median?

2   Implement the procedure from Question 1. What is the percentage of respondents in the 'poor' category?

3   What problem would you anticipate if you used the mean and the range as measures of central tendency and dispersion respectively for the variable 'size of firm' in Table 8.10?

4   Which of the following should *not* be used to represent an interval variable: (a) a boxplot; (b) a stem and leaf display; (c) a bar chart; or (d) a histogram?

5   What is the appropriate SPSS procedure for calculating the inter-quartile range for **satis** (Job Survey data)?

6   What is the inter-quartile range for **satis**?

7   Why might the standard deviation be superior to the inter-quartile range as a measure of dispersion?

Chapter 6

Sampling and statistical significance

In this chapter, we shall be encountering some issues which are fundamental to an appreciation of how people (or whatever is the unit of analysis) should be selected for inclusion in a study and of how it is possible to generalise to the population from which people are selected. These two related issues are concerned with sampling and the statistical significance of results. In examining sampling we shall be examining the procedures for selecting people so that they are representative of the population from which they are selected. The topic of statistical significance raises the issue of how confident we can be that findings relating to a sample of individuals will also be found in the population from which the sample was selected.

SAMPLING

The issue of sampling is important because it is rarely the case that we have sufficient time and resources to conduct research on all of those individuals who could potentially be included in a study. Two points of clarification are relevant at this early stage. We talk about sampling from a population in the introduction to this chapter. It should be recognised that when we sample it is not necessarily people who are being sampled. We can just as legitimately sample other units of analysis such as organisations, schools, local authorities and so on. Second, by a 'population' is meant a discrete group of units of analysis and not just populations in the conventional sense, such as the population of England and Wales. Populations can be populations of towns, of particular groups (for example, all accountants in the UK), of individuals in a firm, or of firms themselves. When we sample, we are selecting units of analysis from a clearly defined population.

Clearly, some populations can be very large, and it is unlikely that all the units in a population can be included because of the considerable time and cost that such an exercise would entail. Sometimes, they can be sufficiently small for all units to be contacted; or if they are not too large, it may be possible to carry out postal questionnaire or telephone interview surveys on a whole population. On the other hand, researchers are very often faced with the need to sample. By and large, researchers will want to form a representative sample, that is, a sample that can be treated as though it were the population. It is rare that perfectly representative samples can be created, but the chances of forming a representative sample can be considerably enhanced by probability sampling. The distinction between probability and non-probability sampling is a basic distinction in discussions of sampling. With probability sampling, each unit of a population has a specifiable probability of inclusion in a sample. In the basic forms of probability sampling, such as simple random samples (see below), each unit will have an equal probability of inclusion.

As an example of a non-probability sampling procedure, consider the following scenario. An interviewer is asked to obtain answers to interview questions from fifty people – twenty-five of each gender. She positions herself in a shopping area in a town at 9.00 a.m. on a Monday and starts interviewing people one by one. Will a representative sample be acquired? While it is not impossible that the sample is representative, there are too many doubts about its representativeness. For example, most people who work will not be shopping; she may have chosen to interview people who were well-dressed; and some people may be more likely than others to use the shops by which she positions herself. In other words, there is a strong chance that the sample is not representative of the people of the town. If the sample is unrepresentative, then our ability to generalise our findings to the population from which it was selected is sharply curtailed. If we do generalise, our inferences may be incorrect. If the sample is heavily biased towards people who do not work, who appeal to the interviewer because of their appearance and who only shop in certain retail outlets, it is likely to be a poor representation of the wider population.

By contrast, probability sampling permits the selection of a sample that should be representative. The following is a discussion of the main types of probability sample that are likely to be encountered.

Simple random sample

The simple random sample is the most basic type of probability sample. Each unit in the population has an equal probability of inclusion in the sample. Like all forms of probability sample, it requires a sampling frame which provides a complete listing of all the units in a population. Let us say that we want a representative sample of 200 non-manual employees from a firm which has 600 non-manual employees. The sample is often denoted n and the population N. A sampling frame is constructed which lists the 600 non-manual employees. Each employee is allocated a number between 1 and N (that is, 600). Each employee has a probability of n/N of being included in the sample, that is, 1 in 3. Individuals will be selected for inclusion on a random basis to ensure that human choice is eliminated from decisions about who should be included and who excluded.

Each individual in the sampling frame is allocated a number 1 to N. The idea is to select n from this list. To ensure that the process is random, a table of random numbers should be consulted. These tables are usually in columns of five-digit numbers. For example, the figures might be:

26938
37025
00352

Since we need to select a number of individuals which is in three digits (that is, 200), only three digits in each five-digit random number should be considered. Let us say that we take the last three digits in each random number, that is, we exclude the first two from consideration. The first case for inclusion would be that numbered 938. However, since the population is only 600, we cannot have a case numbered 938, so this figure is ignored and we proceed to the next random number. The figure 37025 implies that the case numbered 025 will be the first case for inclusion. The person numbered 025 will be the first sampled case. The next will be the person numbered 352, and so on. The process continues until n (that is, 200) units have been selected.

By relying on a random process for the selection of individuals, the possibility of bias in the selection procedure is largely eliminated and the chances of generating a representative sample is enhanced. Sometimes, a systematic sample is selected rather than a simple random sample. With a systematic sample, the selection of individuals is undertaken directly from the sampling frame and without the need to connect random numbers and cases. In the previous example, a random start between 1 and 3 would be made. Let us say that the number is 1. The first case on the sampling frame would be included. Then, every third case would be selected, since 1 in 3 must be sampled. Thus, the fourth, seventh, tenth, thirteenth and so on would be selected. The chief advantage of the systematic sample over the simple random sample is that it obviates the need to plough through a table of random numbers and to tie in each number with a corresponding case. This procedure can be particularly time-consuming when a large sample must be selected. However, in order to select a systematic sample, the researcher must ensure that there is no inherent ordering to the list of cases in the sampling frame, since this would distort the ensuing sample and would probably mean that it was not representative.

Stratified sampling

Stratified sampling is commonly used by social scientists because it can lend an extra ingredient of precision to a simple random or systematic sample. When selecting a stratified sample, the researcher divides the population into strata. The strata must be categories of a criterion. For example, the population may be stratified according to the criterion of gender, in which case two strata – male and female – will be generated. Alternatively, the criterion may be department in the firm, resulting in possibly five strata: production, marketing, personnel, accounting, and research and development. Provided that the information is readily available, people are grouped into the strata. A simple random or systematic sample is then taken from the listing in each stratum. It is important for the stratifying criterion to be relevant to the issues in which the researcher is interested; it should not be undertaken for its own sake. The researcher may be interested in how the attitudes of non-manual employees are affected by the department in the firm to which they are attached. The advantage of stratified sampling is that it offers the possibility of greater accuracy, by ensuring that the groups which are created by a stratifying criterion are represented in the same proportions as in the population.

Table 6.1 provides an illustration of the idea of a stratified sample. The table provides the numbers of non-manual personnel in each department in the first column and the number of each department (that is, stratum) that would be selected on a 1 in 3 basis. The important point to note is that the proportions of personnel from each department in the sample are the same as in the population. The largest department – production – has 35 per cent of all non-manual employees in the firm and 35 per cent of non-manual employees in the sample. A simple random or systematic sample without stratification might have achieved the same result, but a stratified sample greatly enhances the likelihood of the proper representation of strata in the sample. Two or more stratifying criteria can be employed in tandem. For example, if the researcher were interested in the effects of gender on job attitudes, as well as belonging to different departments, we would then have ten strata (five departments × two sexes), that is, men and women in production, men and women in marketing, and so on. A 1 in 3 sample would then be taken from each of the ten strata.

If the numbers in some strata are likely to be small, it may be necessary to sample disproportionately. For example, we may sample 2 in 3 of those in Research and Development. This would mean that thirty, rather than fifteen, would be sampled from this department. However, to compensate for the extra fifteen individuals sampled in Research and Development, slightly fewer than 1 in 3 in Production and in Accounting may need to be sampled. When this occurs, it has to be recognised that the sample is differentially weighted relative to the population, so that estimates of the sample mean will have to be corrected to reflect this weighting.

Multistage cluster sampling

One disadvantage of the probability samples covered so far is that they do not deal very well with geographically dispersed populations. If we took a simple random sample of all chartered accountants in the UK or indeed of the population of the UK itself, the resulting sample would be highly scattered. If the aim were to conduct an interview survey, interviewers would spend a great deal of time and money travelling to their respondents. A multistage cluster sample is a probability sampling procedure that allows such geographically dispersed populations to be adequately covered, while simultaneously saving interviewer time and travel costs.

Initially, the researcher samples clusters, that is, areas of the geographical region being covered. The case of seeking to sample households in a very large city

Table 6.1 Devising a stratified random sample:
          non-manual employees in a firm

Department	Population N	Sample n
Production	210	70
Marketing	120	40
Personnel	63	21
Accounting	162	54
Research and development	45	15
Total	600	200

can be taken as an example of the procedure. At the first stage, all the electoral wards in the city would be ascribed a number from 1 to N and a simple random sample of wards selected. At the second stage, a simple random sample of streets in each ward might be taken. At the third stage, a simple random sample of households in the sampled streets would be selected from the list of addresses in the electoral rolls for the relevant wards. By concentrating interviewers in small regions of the city, much time and travel cost can be saved. Very often, stratification accompanies the sampling of clusters. For example, wards might be categorised in terms of an indicator of economic prosperity (for example, high, medium and low) such as the percentage of heads of household in professional and managerial jobs. Stratification will ensure that clusters are properly represented in terms of this criterion.

SAMPLING PROBLEMS

One of the most frequently asked questions in the context of sampling is: How large should a sample be? In reality, there can only be a few guidelines to answering this question, rather than a single definitive response.

First, the researcher almost always works within time and resource constraints, so that decisions about sample size must always recognise these boundaries. There is no point in working out an ideal sample size for a project if you have nowhere near the amount of resources required to bring it into effect. Second, the larger the sample the greater the accuracy. Contrary to expectations, the size of the sample relative to the size of the population (in other words n/N) is rarely relevant to the issue of a sample's accuracy. This means that sampling error – differences between the sample and the population which are due to sampling – can be reduced by increasing sampling size. However, after a certain level, increases in accuracy tend to tail off as sample size increases, so that greater accuracy becomes economically unacceptable.

Third, the problem of non-response should be borne in mind. Most sample surveys attract a certain amount of non-response. Thus, it is likely that only some of the 200 non-manual employees we sample will agree to participate in the research. If it is our aim to ensure as far as possible that 200 employees are interviewed and if we think that there may be a 20 per cent rate of non-response, it may be advisable to select 250 individuals, on the grounds that approximately 50 will be non-respondents. Finally, the researcher should bear in mind the kind of analysis he or she intends to undertake. For example, if the researcher intends to examine the relationship between department in the firm and attitudes to white-collar unions, a table in which department is cross-tabulated against attitude can be envisaged. If 'attitude to white-collar unions' comprises four answers and since 'department' comprises five categories, a table of twenty 'cells' would be engendered (see discussion of contingency tables and cross-tabulation in Chapter 8). In order for there to be an adequate number of cases in each cell a fairly large sample will be required. Consequently, considerations of sample size should be sensitive to the kinds of analysis that will subsequently be required.

The issue of non-response draws attention to the fact that a well-crafted sample can be jeopardised by the failure of individuals to participate. The problem is that respondents and non-respondents may differ from each other in certain respects, so respondents may not be representative of the population. Sometimes, researchers try to discern whether respondents are disproportionately drawn from particular groups, such as whether men are clearly more inclined not to participate than women. However, such tests can only be conducted in relation to fairly superficial characteristics like gender; deeper differences, such as attitudinal ones, cannot readily be tested. In addition, some members of a sample may not be contactable, because they have moved or are on holiday. Moreover, even when a questionnaire is answered, there may still be questions which, by design or error, are not answered. Each of these three elements – non-response, inability to contact and missing information for certain variables – may be a source of bias, since we do not know how representative those who do respond to each variable are of the population.

Finally, although social scientists are well aware of the advantages of probability sampling procedures, a great deal of research does not derive from probability samples. In a review of 126 articles in the field of organisation studies which were based on correlational research, Mitchell (1985) found that only twenty-one were based on probability samples. The rest used convenience samples, that is, samples which are either 'chosen' by the investigator or which choose themselves (for example, volunteers). However, when it is borne in mind that response rates to sample surveys are often quite low and are declining (Goyder, 1988), the difference between research based on random samples and convenience samples in terms of their relative representativeness is not always as great as is sometimes implied. None the less, many of the statistical tests and procedures to be encountered later in this book assume that the data derive from a random sample. The point being made here is that this requirement is often not fulfilled, and that even when a random sample has been used, factors like non-response may adversely affect its random qualities.

STATISTICAL SIGNIFICANCE

How do we know if a sample is typical or representative of the population from which it has been drawn? To find this out we need to be able to describe the nature of the sample and the population. This is done in terms of the distributions of their values. Thus, for example, if we wanted to find out whether the proportion of men to women in our sample was similar to that in some specified population, we would compare the two proportions. The main tests for tackling such problems are described in Chapters 7 and 9. It should be noted that the same principle lies behind all statistical tests, including those concerned with describing the relationship between two or more variables. Here, the basic idea underlying them will be outlined.

To do this we shall take the simple case of wanting to discover whether a coin was unbiased in the sense that it lands heads and tails an equal number of times. The number of times we tossed the coin would constitute the sample while the population would be the outcomes we would theoretically expect if the coin were unbiased. If we flipped the coin just once, then the probability of it turning up heads is once every two throws, or 0.5. In other words, we would have to toss it at least twice to determine if both possibilities occur. If we were to do this, however, there would be four possible theoretical outcomes, as shown in Table 6.2: (1) a tail followed by a head; (2) a head followed by a tail; (3) two tails; and (4) two heads. What happens on each throw is *independent* of, or not affected by, the outcome of any other throw. If the coin were unbiased, then each of the four outcomes would be equally probable. In other words, the probability of obtaining either two tails or two heads (but not both possibilities) is one in four, or 0.25, while that of obtaining a head and a tail is two in four, or 0.5. The probability of obtaining a head and a tail (0.5) is greater than that of two tails (0.25) or two heads (0.25) but is the same as that for two tails and two heads combined (0.25+0.25). From this it should be clear that it is not possible to draw conclusions about a coin being unbiased from so few throws or such a small sample. This is because the frequency of improbable events is much greater with smaller samples. Consequently, it is much more difficult with such samples to determine whether they come from a certain population.

If we plot or draw the distribution of the probability of obtaining the same proportion of heads to tails as shown in Figure 6.1, then it will take the shape of an inverted 'V'. This shape contains all the possible outcomes which add up to 1 (0.25+0.25+0.25+0.25=1).

Table 6.2 Four possible outcomes of tossing a coin twice

Possible outcomes		Probability (p)
1 Head Tail		0.25 ⎫
2 Tail Head		0.25 ⎬ = 0.5
3 Head Head		0.25
4 Tail Tail		0.25

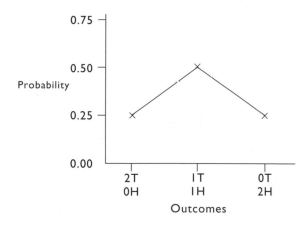

Figure 6.1 The distribution of similar theoretical outcomes of tossing a coin
twice

Theoretically, the more often we throw the coin, the more similar the distribution of the possible outcomes will be to an inverted 'U' or normal distribution. Suppose, for example, we threw the same coin six times (or, what amounts to the same thing, six coins once). If we did this, there would be sixty-four possible outcomes. These are shown in Table 6.3. The total number of outcomes can be calculated by multiplying the number of possible outcomes on each occasion (2) by those of the other occasions ($2 \times 2 \times 2 \times 2 \times 2 \times 2 = 64$). The probability of obtain-

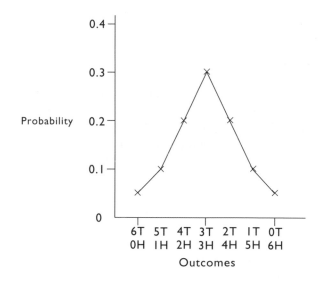

Figure 6.2 The distribution of similar theoretical outcomes of tossing a coin six
times

Table 6.3 Theoretical outcomes of tossing a coin six times and the probabilities of similar outcomes

	Theoretical outcomes	Probability		Theoretical outcomes	Probability
1	TTTTTT	0.016	64	HHHHHH	0.016
2	TTTTTH		63	HHHHHT	
3	TTTTHT		62	HHHHTH	
4	TTTHTT	0.094	61	HHHTHH	0.094
5	TTHTTT		60	HHTHHH	
6	THTTTT		59	HTHHHH	
7	HTTTTT		58	THHHHH	
8	TTTTHH		57	HHHHTT	
9	TTTHHT		56	HHHTTH	
10	TTHHTT		55	HHTTHH	
11	TTTHTH		54	HHHTHT	
12	TTHTHT		53	HHTHTH	
13	TTHTTH		52	HHTHHT	
14	THTHTT		51	HTHTHH	
15	THHTTT	0.234	50	HTTHHH	0.234
16	THTTTH		49	HTHHHT	
17	THTTHT		48	HTHHTH	
18	HTTHTT		47	THHTHH	
19	HTTTHT		46	THHHTH	
20	HTHTTT		45	THTHHH	
21	HTTTTH		44	THHHHT	
22	HHTTTT		43	TTHHHH	
23	TTTHHH		42	HHHTTT	
24	TTHHHT		41	HHTTTH	
25	TTHHTH		40	HHTTHT	
26	TTHTHH		39	HHTHTT	
27	THTHTH		38	HTHTHT	
28	THTHHT		37	HTHTTH	0.312
29	THHTTH		36	HTTHHT	
30	THHTHT		35	HTTHTH	
31	THTTHH		34	HTHHTT	
32	THHHTT		33	HTTTHH	

ing six heads or six tails in a row (but not both) would be 1 in 64 or about 0.016. Since there are six possible ways in which one head and five tails can be had, the probability of achieving this is 6 out of 64 or about 0.10 (that is, 0.016×6). The distribution of the probability of obtaining different sequences of the same number of tails and heads grouped together (for example, the six sequences of finding five tails and a head) is presented in Figure 6.2.

It should be clear from this discussion that we can never be 100 per cent certain that the coin is unbiased, because even if we threw it 1,000 times, there is a very small chance that it will turn up all heads or all tails on every one of those throws. So what we do is to set a criterion or cut-off point at or beyond which we assume the coin will be judged to be biased. This point is arbitrary and is referred to as the *significance level*. It is usually set at a probability or p level of 0.05, or five times out of a hundred. Since the coin can be biased in one of two ways, that is, in favour of either heads or tails, this 5 per cent is shared equally between these two possibilities. This means, in effect, that the probability of the coin being biased towards heads will be 0.025 and that the probability of its bias towards tails will also be 0.025. In other words, if it turns up heads or tails six times in a row, then the probability of both these outcomes occurring would be about 0.032 (that is, 0.016+0.016), which is below the probability of 0.05. If either of these two events were to happen we would accept that the coin was biased. If, however, it landed tails once and heads five times, or heads once and tails five times, there are six ways in which either of these two outcomes could happen. Consequently, the probability of either one happening is 6 out of 64, or about 0.10. The probability of both outcomes occurring is about 0.2 (that is, 0.10+0.10). In this case, we would have to accept that the coin was unbiased, since this probability level is above the criterion of 0.05.

Because we can never be 100 per cent certain that the coin is either biased or unbiased, we can make one of two kinds of error. The first kind is to decide that the coin is biased when it is not. This is known as a *Type I error* and is sometimes referred to as α (alpha). For example, as we have seen, an unbiased coin may land heads six times in a row. The second kind of error is to judge the coin to be unbiased when it is biased. This is called a *Type II error* and is represented by β (beta). It is possible, for instance, for a biased coin to come up tails once and heads five times. We can reduce the possibility of making a Type I error by accepting a lower level of significance, say 0.01 instead of 0.05. But doing this increases the probability of making a Type II error. In other words, the probability of a Type I error is inversely related to that of a Type II one. The more likely we are to make a Type I error, the less likely we are to commit a Type II error.

At this stage, it is useful to discuss briefly three kinds of probability distribution. The first is known as a *binomial* distribution and is based on the idea that if only either of two outcomes can occur on any one occasion (for example, heads or tails if a coin is thrown), then we can work out the theoretical distribution of the different combinations of outcomes which could occur if we knew the number of occasions that had taken place. One characteristic of this distribution is that it consists of a limited or finite number of events. If, however, we threw an infinite number of coins an infinite number of times, then we would have a distribution which would consist of an infinite possibility of events. This distribution is known variously as a DeMoivre's, Gaussian, standard normal or z curve distribution. If random samples of these probabilities are taken and plotted, then the shape of those distributions will depend on the size of the samples. Smaller samples will produce flatter distributions with thicker tails than the normal distribution, while larger ones will be very similar to it. These distributions are known as t distributions. What this means is that when we want to know the likelihood that a particular series of events could have occurred by chance, we need to take into account the size of the sample on which those events are based.

So far, in order to convey the idea that certain events may occur just by chance, we have used the example of tossing a coin. Although this may seem a bit remote from the kinds of data we collect in the social sciences, we use this underlying principle to determine issues such as whether a sample is representative of its population and whether two or more samples or treatments differ from each other. Suppose we draw a small sample of six people and want to determine if the proportion of males to females in it is similar to that of the population in which the number of men and women are equal. Each person can only be male or female. Since there are six people, there are sixty-four possible outcomes (that is, $2 \times 2 \times 2 \times 2 \times 2 \times 2$). These, of course, are the same as those displayed in Table 6.3 except that we now substitute males for tails and females for heads. The joint probability of all six people being either male or female would be about 0.03 (that is, $0.016+0.016$), so that if this were the result we would reject the notion that the sample was representative of the population. However, if one was male and the other five female, or there was one female and five males, then the probability of this occurring by chance would be about 0.2 (that is, $0.096 + 0.096$). This would mean that at the 0.05 significance level we would accept either of these two outcomes or samples as being typical of the population because the probability of obtaining these outcomes is greater than the 0.05 level. This shows that sample values can diverge quite widely from those of their populations and still be drawn from them, although it should be emphasised that this outcome would be less frequent the larger the sample. Statistical tests which compare a sample with a population are known as *one-sample tests* and can be found in the next chapter.

The same principle underlies tests which have been developed to find out if two or more samples or treatments come from the same population or different ones, although this is a little more difficult to grasp. For example, we may be interested in finding out whether women are more perceptive than men, or whether alcohol impairs performance. In the first case, the two samples are women and men while in the second they are alcohol and no alcohol. Once again, in order to explain the idea that underlies these tests, it may be useful to think about it initially in terms of throwing a coin, except that this time we throw two coins. The two coins represent the two samples. We want to know whether the two coins differ in their tendency to be unbiased. If the two coins were unbiased and if we were to throw them six times each, then we should expect the two sets of theoretical outcomes obtained to be the same as that in Table 6.3. In other words, the two distributions should overlap each other exactly.

Now if we threw the two coins six times each, it is unlikely that the empirical outcomes would be precisely the same, even if the coins were unbiased. In fact, we can work out the theoretical probability of the two distributions being different in the same way as we did earlier for the coin turning up heads or tails. It may be easier in the first instance if we begin by comparing the outcomes of tossing two coins just once. If we do this, there are four possible outcomes: (1) two tails; (2) two heads; (3) one tail and one head; and (4) one head and one tail. If we look at these outcomes in terms of whether they are the same or different, then two of them are the same (two tails and two heads) while two of them are different (one tail and one head, and vice versa). In other words, the probability of finding a difference is two out of four, or 0.5, which is the same as that for discovering no difference. We stand an equal chance of finding no difference as we do of a difference if we throw two unbiased coins once.

Thinking solely in terms of the outcomes of the two coins being the same or different, if we threw the two coins twice, then there would be four possible outcomes: (1) two the same; (2) two different; (3) the first the same and the second different; and (4) the first different and the second the same. In other words, the probability of obtaining the same outcome when two unbiased coins are thrown twice is 0.25. The probability of the outcomes being mixed is greater with the value being 0.5. The probability of the outcomes being the same on all six throws would be about 0.016 ($0.5 \times 0.5 \times 0.5 \times 0.5 \times 0.5 \times 0.5 = 0.016$). Hence, if the two coins were unbiased, we would not expect them to give the same outcome on each occasion they were tossed. The distribution of the outcomes of the two coins represents, in effect, what we would expect to happen if the differences between two samples or two treatments were due to chance.

Applying this idea to the kind of question that may be asked in the social sciences, we may wish to find out if women and men differ in their perceptiveness. There are three possible answers to this question: (1) women may be more perceptive than men; (2) they may be no different from them; or (3) they may be less perceptive than them. In other words, we can have three different expectations or hypotheses about what the answer might be. Not expecting any difference is known as the *null hypothesis*. Anticipating a difference but not being able to predict what it is likely to be is called a *non-directional hypothesis*. However, it is unlikely that we would ask this sort of question if we did not expect a difference of a particular nature, since there are an infinite number of such questions which can be posed. In carrying out research we are often concerned with showing that a particular relationship either holds or does not hold between two or more variables. In other words, we are examining the direction as well as the existence of a relationship. In this case, we may be testing the idea that women are more perceptive than men. This would be an example of a *directional hypothesis*. As we shall see, specifying the direction of the hypothesis means that we can adopt a slightly higher and more lenient level of significance.

Since there are three possible outcomes (that is, a probability of 0.33 for any one outcome) for each paired comparison, if we tested this hypothesis on a small sample of five men and five women, then the probability of all five women being more perceptive than men just by chance would be about 0.004 (that is, $0.33 \times 0.33 \times 0.33 \times 0.33 \times 0.33$). If we obtained this result, and if we adopted the usual 0.05 or 5 per cent as the significance level at or below which this finding is unlikely to be due to chance, then we would accept the hypothesis since 0.004 is less than 0.05. In other words, we would state that women were significantly more perceptive than men below the 5 per cent level – see Figure 6.3(a). As we shall see, SPSS usually provides the exact level of significance for each test. It has been customary in the social sciences to provide the significance level only for results which fall at or below the 0.05 level and to do so for certain cut-off points below that such as 0.01, 0.001, and 0.0001. However, with the advent of computer programs such as SPSS which give exact significance levels, it could be argued that this tradition does not maximise the information that could be supplied without any obvious disadvantages.

If, however, we found that only four of the women were more perceptive than the men, then the probability of this happening by chance would be about 0.04, since there are ten ways or sequences in which this result could occur ($0.004 \times 10 = 0.04$). This finding is still significant. However, if we had adopted a non-directional hypothesis and had simply expected a difference between men and women without specifying its direction, then this result would not be significant at the 0.05 level since this 0.05 would have to be shared between both tails of the distribution of possible outcomes as in Figure 6.3 (b). In other words, it would become 0.025 at either end of the distribution. This result would require a probability level of 0.025 or less to be significant when stated as a non-directional

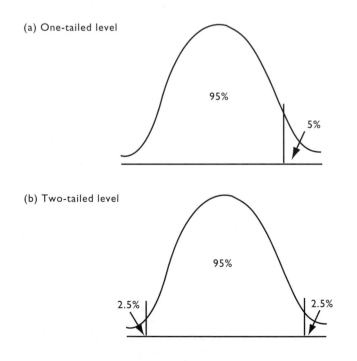

Figure 6.3 One-tailed and two-tailed 0.05 levels of significance

Table 6.4 Type I and Type II errors

		Reality	
		No difference	A difference
Interpretation of reality	Accept no difference	Correct	Type II error β
	Accept a difference	Type I error α	Correct

hypothesis. As it is, the probability of either four women being more perceptive than men or four men being more perceptive than women is the sum of these two probabilities, namely 0.08, which is above the 0.05 level. The important point to note is that non-directional hypotheses require *two-tailed* significance levels while directional hypotheses only need *one-tailed* ones. If we find a difference between two samples or treatments we did not expect, then to test the significance of this result we need to use a two-tailed test.

It may be worth reiterating at this stage that a finding of four out of the five women being more perceptive than the five men may still be obtained by chance even at the 0.04 one-tailed level. In other words, this means that there remains a 4 in 100 possibility that this result could be due to chance. In accepting this level of significance for rejecting the null hypothesis that there is no difference between men and women, we may be committing a Type I error, namely thinking that there is a difference between them when in fact there is no such difference. In other words, a Type I error is rejecting the null hypothesis when it is true, as shown in Table 6.4. We may reduce the probability of making this kind of error by lowering the significance level from 0.05 to 0.01, but this increases the probability of committing a Type II error, which is accepting that there is no difference when there is one. A Type II error is accepting the null hypothesis when it is false. Setting the significance level at 0.01 means that the finding that four out of the five women are more perceptive than the men is assuming that this result is due to chance when it may be indicating a real difference.

The probability of correctly assuming that there is a difference when there actually is one is known as the *power* of a test. A powerful test is one that is more likely to indicate a significant difference when such a difference exists. Statistical power is inversely related to the probability of making a Type II error and is calculated by subtracting beta from one (that is, $1-\beta$).

Finally, it is important to realise that the level of significance has nothing to do with the size or importance of a difference. It is simply concerned with the probability of that difference arising by chance. In other words, a difference between two samples or two treatments which is significant at the 0.05 level is not necessarily bigger than one which is significant at the 0.0001 level. The latter difference is only less probable than the former one.

Inferring from samples to populations

The section so far has raised the prospect of being able to generalise from a sample to a population. We can never know for sure whether a characteristic we find in a sample applies to the population from which the sample was randomly selected. As the discussion so far suggests, what we can do is to estimate the degree of confidence we can have in the characteristic we find. If we find, as we did in Chapter 5, that the mean income in the Job Survey is £15,638.24, how confident can we be that this is the mean income for the population of workers in the firm as a whole?

A crucial consideration in determining the degree of confidence that we can have in a mean based on a sample of the population is the *standard error of the mean*, which is the standard deviation of the sample means. This notion is based on the following considerations. The sample that we select is one of only an incredibly large number of random samples that could have been selected. Some of these samples would find a mean that is the same as the population mean, some will be very close to it (either above or below) and some will be further away from it (again, either above or below the population mean). If we have a population that is normally distributed, the distribution of all possible sample means will also be normally distributed. This suggests that most sample means will be the same as or close to the population mean, but that some will deviate from it by quite a large amount. The standard error of the mean expresses the degree of dispersion of these means. We know from the discussion in Chapter 5 concerning the attributes of a normal distribution that 95.44 per cent of all cases lie within two standard deviations of the population mean. More precisely, we know that 95 per cent of cases lie within a range that is plus or minus 1.96 standard deviations of the mean. Since the distribution of sample means is normally distributed around the population mean, we can deduce that 95 per cent of all samples lie within a range that is plus or minus 1.96 standard errors from the population mean. Needless to say, the corollary of this is that 5 per cent of samples lie outside that range. This is likely to occur when there is a high level of sampling error.

This reasoning becomes important in research because we can infer the upper and lower levels of range within which the population mean falls. This range is known as the *confidence interval*. We can infer that there is a 95 per cent chance that the population mean will lie between the sample mean plus or minus 1.96 standard errors of the mean. In fact, we can see from Table 5.6 that not only does SPSS provide the standard error of the mean (242.04), it also gives us the 95 per cent confidence intervals. We can be 95 per cent confident that the population mean will lie between £15,155.13 and £16,121.34. It is always possible that the mean that you find in your research is based on a highly unrepresentative sample and is therefore one of the 5 per cent of sample means falling outside the range of plus or minus 1.96 standard errors of the population mean. Essentially, we are taking a gamble that our sample mean is one of the 95 per cent that lies within the range.

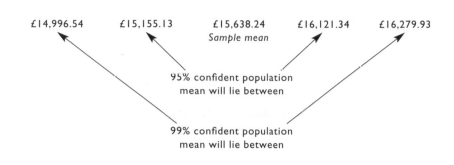

Figure 6.4 Confidence intervals

The standard error of the mean is calculated by dividing the standard deviation (which in this case is 1995.89) by the square root of the sample size (68). As this calculation implies, the more dispersed the sample is around the mean (that is, the larger the standard deviation), the larger the sample error of the mean will be. This in turn means that the confidence interval range will be larger.

A further consideration is that there may be research issues where you need to be more than 95 per cent confident that the population mean lies within the confidence interval. For the bulk of social issues, the 95 per cent level of confidence is adequate, but there may be occasions when you need to be more confident. If, for example, you wanted to be 99 per cent confident that the population mean fell within the confidence interval, a wider range of upper and lower values would need to be specified. This is calculated as the sample mean plus or minus 2.58 standard errors of the mean. When you use **Explore** to provide confidence interval information, it uses the 95 per cent confidence level as a default selection. To change the default confidence level, while in the **Explore** dialog box (Box 5.8):

→**Statistics…** [opens **Explore: Statistics** subdialog box]
change **Confidence Interval for Mean:** from **95** to **99** % →**Continue** [closes **Explore: Statistics** subdialog box]
→**OK**

The confidence interval is then £14996.54 to £16279.93. It means that you can be 99 per cent confident that the population mean lies within that range. Figure 6.4 attempts to capture these ideas.

EXERCISES

1   What is the difference between a random sample and a representative sample?
2   Why might a stratified sample be superior to a simple random sample?
3   In what context might multistage cluster sampling be particularly useful?

4   If a sample of grocery shops were selected randomly from the Yellow Pages directory for your town, would you necessarily have a representative sample?

5   Flip a coin four times. What is the probability of finding the particular sequence of outcomes you found?

6   If the coin were unbiased, would you obtain two heads and two tails if you threw it four times?

7   What is the probability of obtaining any sequence of two heads and two tails?

8   You have developed a test of general knowledge which consists of a hundred statements, half of which are false and half of which are true. Each person is given one point for a correct answer. How many points is someone who has no general knowledge most likely to achieve on this test?

9   Fifty people are tested to see if they can tell margarine from butter. Half of them are given butter and the other half are given margarine. They have to say which of these two products they were given (that is, there were no 'don't knows'). If people cannot discriminate between them, how many people on average are likely to guess correctly?

10   If we wanted to see if women were more talkative than men, what would the null hypothesis be?

11   What would the non-directional hypothesis be?

12   What is the 95 per cent confidence interval for **age** in the Job Survey?

Chapter 7

Bivariate analysis

Exploring differences between scores on two variables

In this chapter we shall be looking at ways of determining whether the differences between the distributions of two variables are statistically significant. Thus, for example, when analysing data we may wish to know the answers to some of the following kinds of questions: Is the proportion of black to white workers the same among men as it is among women? Do women workers earn less than their male counterparts? Does job satisfaction change from one month to the next? Do the scores in one treatment group differ from those in another?

In looking at differences between two variables, the variable which we use to form our comparison groups usually has a small number of values or levels, say between two and six. We shall call this the comparison-group variable to distinguish it from the other one, which we shall refer to as the criterion variable. The comparison variable is sometimes known as the *independent* variable, and the criterion variable as the *dependent* one. An example of a comparison-group variable is gender if we want to compare men with women. This typically has two levels (that is, men and women) which go to make up two comparison groups. Race or ethnic origin, on the other hand, may take on two or more levels (for example, Caucasian, Negroid, Asian, and Mongolian), thereby creating two or more comparison groups. Other examples of comparison-group variables include different experimental treatments (for example, drugs versus psychotherapy in treating depression), different points in time (for example, two consecutive months), and the categorisation of participants into various levels on some variable (such as high, intermediate and low job satisfaction). The other variable is the one that we shall use to make our comparison (for example, income or job satisfaction).

CRITERIA FOR SELECTING BIVARIATE TESTS OF DIFFERENCES

There are a relatively large number of statistical tests to determine whether a difference between two or more groups is significant. In deciding which is the most appropriate statistical test to use to analyse your data, it is necessary to bear the following considerations in mind.

Categorical data

If the data are of a categorical or nominal nature, where the values refer to the number or frequency of cases that fall within particular categories such as the number of black female workers, it is only possible to use what is referred to as a *non-parametric* test (see below for an explanation). Thus, for example, in trying to determine whether there are significantly more white than black female employees, it would be necessary to use a non-parametric test.

Ordinal and interval/ratio data

If the data are of a non-categorical nature, such as the rating of how skilled workers are or how much they earn, then it is necessary to decide whether it is more appropriate to use a *parametric* or *non-parametric* test. This issue is a complex and controversial one which will be discussed later in some detail.

Means or variances?

Most investigators who use parametric tests are primarily interested in checking for differences between means. Differences in *variances* are also normally carried out but only to determine the appropriateness of using such a test to check for differences in the means. Variance is an expression showing the spread or dispersion of data around the mean and is the square of the standard deviation. If the variances are found to differ markedly, then it may be more appropriate to use a non-parametric test. However, differences in variance (that is, variability) may be of interest in their own right and so these tests have been listed separately. Thus, for example, it may be reasonable to suppose that the variability of job satisfaction of women will be greater than that of men, but that there will be no difference in their mean scores. In this case, it would also be necessary to pay attention to the differences between the variances to determine if this is so.

Related or unrelated comparison groups?

Which test you use also depends on whether the values that you want to compare come from different cases or from the same or similar ones. If, for example, you are comparing different groups of people, such as men and women or people who have been assigned to different experimental treatments, then you are dealing with unrelated samples of participants. It is worth noting that this kind of situation or design is also referred to in some of the following other ways: *independent* or *uncorrelated* groups or samples; and *between-subjects* design. If, on the other hand, you are comparing the way that the same people have responded on separate occasions or under different conditions, then you are dealing with *related* samples of observations. This is also true of groups of people who are or have been *matched* or *paired* on one or more important characteristics, for example, husbands and wives, which may also make them more similar in terms of the criterion variable under study. Once again, there are a number of other terms used to describe related scores such as the following: *dependent* or *correlated* groups or samples; *repeated measures*; and *within-subjects* design.

Two or more comparison groups?

Different tests are generally used to compare two rather than three or more comparison groups.

The tests to be used given these criteria are listed in Table 7.1. Readers may wish to use this table as a guide to the selection of tests appropriate to their needs. Page numbers are inserted in the table cells to facilitate finding the appropriate tests.

PARAMETRIC VERSUS NON-PARAMETRIC TESTS

One of the unresolved issues in data analysis is the question of when parametric rather than non-parametric tests should be used. Some writers have argued that it is only appropriate to use parametric tests when the data fulfil the following three conditions:

1   the level or scale of measurement is of equal interval or ratio scaling, that is, more than ordinal;
2   the distribution of the population scores is normal; and
3   the variances of both variables are equal or *homogeneous*.

The term *parameter* refers to a measure which describes the distribution of the population such as the mean or variance. Since parametric tests are based on the assumption that we know certain characteristics of the population from which the sample is drawn, they are called *parametric tests*. *Non-parametric* or *distribution-free* tests are so named because they do not depend on assumptions about the precise form of the distribution of the sampled populations.

However, the need to meet these three conditions for using parametric tests has been strongly questioned. Some of the arguments will be mentioned here and these will be simply stated, with sources provided where further details can be found. As far as the first condition is concerned, level of measurement, it has been suggested that parametric tests can also be used with ordinal variables since tests apply to numbers and not to what those numbers signify (for example, Lord, 1953). Thus, for example, we apply these tests to determine if two scores differ. We know what these scores indicate, but the test obviously does not. Therefore, the data are treated as if they are of interval or ratio scaling. Furthermore, it can be argued that since many psychological and sociological variables such as attitudes are basically ordinal in nature (see p. 58), parametric tests should not be used to analyse them if this first condition is valid. However, it should be noted that parametric tests are routinely applied to such variables.

Table 7.1 Tests of differences

Nature of criterion variable	Type of test	Type of data	Number of comparison groups	Name of test	Page numbers
Categorical: nominal or frequency	Non-parametric	Unrelated	1	Binomial	117–19
			1	Chi-square	119–22
		Related	2+	Chi-square	122–5
			2	McNemar	126–7
			3+	Cochran Q	128
Non-categorical:	Non-parametric	Unrelated	1–2	Kolmogorov–Smirnov	128–31
			2	Mann–Whitney U	133–4
			2+	Median	131–3
			3+	Kruskal–Wallis H	134–5
		Related	2	Sign	135–6
			2	Wilcoxon	137
			3+	Friedman	138
	Parametric: means	Unrelated	1–2	t	138–43
			2+	One-way and two-way analysis of variance	144–7, 205–7, 214–17
		Related	2	t	149–51
			2+	Single factor repeated measures	152–6
		Related and unrelated	2+	Two-way analysis of variance with repeated measures on one factor	218–21
			2+	Two-way analysis of covariance	210–13
	Parametric: variances	Unrelated	2+	Levene's test	142–3, 146
		Related	2	t	152

With respect to the second and third conditions, the populations being normally distributed and of equal variances, a number of studies have been carried out (for example, Boneau, 1960; Games and Lucas, 1966) where the values of the statistics used to analyse samples drawn from populations which have been artificially set up to violate these conditions have been found not to differ greatly from those for samples which have been drawn from populations which do not violate these conditions. Tests which are able to withstand such violations are described as being *robust*.

One exception to this general finding is where both the size of the samples and the variances are unequal, although some have argued that this exception applies even with equal sample sizes (Wilcox, 1987). Another exception is where both distributions of scores are non-normal. In such circumstances, it may be prudent to compare the results of a non-parametric test with those of a parametric test. Where the distributions of scores are not normal, it may also be worth running a parametric test on the scores as they are and after they have been transformed closer to normality. For more details on transforming scores to normality, see Mosteller and Tukey (1977). It may also be more desirable to use non-parametric tests when the size of the samples is small, say under fifteen, since under these circumstances it is more difficult to determine the extent to which these conditions have been met. A fuller description of non-parametric tests may be found in Siegel and Castellan (1988) or Conover (1980).

CATEGORICAL VARIABLES AND NON-PARAMETRIC TESTS

Binomial test for one dichotomous variable

The binomial test is used to compare the frequency of cases actually found in the two categories of a dichotomous variable with those which are expected on some basis. Suppose, for example, that we want to find out whether the ratio of female to male workers in the industry covered by our Job Survey is the same as that in the industry in general, which we know to be 1:3. We could do this by carrying out a binomial test in which the proportion of women in our survey is compared with that of an expected proportion of 1:4 or one out of every four workers.

To do this with SPSS, we would use the following sequence:

→**Analyze** →**Nonparametric Tests** →**Binomial...** [opens **Binomial Test** dialog box shown in Box 7.1]
→**gender** →▶button [puts **gender** under **Test Variable List:**] →box called **Test Proportion:** and type **.75** →**OK**

Since males have been coded as 1, they form the first category and the proportion of them becomes 3:4, or 0.75. The default value is 0.5. The two categories

Binomial Test

ethnicgp	Test Variable List:
income	gender
age	
years	
commit	
satis1	
satis2	
satis3	

Define Dichotomy
- ⦿ Get from data
- ◯ Cut point: [ ]

Test Proportion: [.750]

Buttons: OK, Paste, Reset, Cancel, Help, Exact..., Options...

Box 7.1 **Binomial Test** dialog box

compared are taken from the data by default (**Get from data**) so the lower category (for example, **1**) of a dichotomous variable such as **gender** forms one group and the higher category (for example, **2**) the other group. If there are more than two groups (such as in **ethnicgp**) and we wish to compare two of them (such as Asian and West Indian workers), we would have to select these two groups. Sometimes it may be possible to define our two groups by using a cut-off point. For instance, if we wished to determine if there were equal numbers of black and white workers, we could do this by typing **1** in the box entitled **Cut point:**. All cases equal to or less than this point form the first category, while all the others form the second category.

The output for the first procedure is displayed in Table 7.2. (It should be noted that there are no zeros before the decimal points; this reflects a general tendency in SPSS that where the maximum value is one, there is no zero before the decimal point.) As we can see, the number of males (thirty-nine) is only slightly greater than that of females (thirty-one) and so it would appear from an inspection of these

Table 7.2 Binomial test comparing proportion of men and women (Job Survey)

Binomial Test

		Category	N	Observed Prop.	Test Prop.	Asymp. Sig. (1-tailed)
GENDER	Group 1	1	39	.56	.75	.000[a]
	Group 2	2	31	.44		
	Total		70	1.00		

a. Alternative hypothesis states that the proportion of cases in the first group < .75.

b. Based on Z Approximation.

Table 7.3 Binomial test comparing proportion of whites and non-whites
(Job Survey)

Binomial Test

		Category	N	Observed Prop.	Test Prop.	Asymp. Sig. (2-tailed)
ETHNICGP	Group 1	<=1	36	.51	.50	.905[a]
	Group 2	> 1	34	.49		
	Total		70	1.00		

a. Based on Z Approximation.

figures that the ratio of males to females is nearer 1:1 than 3:1. The hypothesis that the proportion of males to females is 0.75 is rejected since the probability of obtaining this result by chance is highly unlikely with p equal to 0.000. SPSS gives p to three decimal places. Where, as in this case, p consists of three zeros, the fourth decimal place is 5, which means that p is at least 0.0005. Consequently, the difference between the obtained and hypothesised outcome is interpreted as being statistically different. Therefore, we would conclude that the ratio of male to female workers is not 3:1.

The output for comparing the proportion of white and non-white workers is shown in Table 7.3. The number of white workers (thirty-six) is almost the same as that of non-white ones (thirty-four), so the ratio is close to 1:1. The hypothesis that there are equal numbers of white and non-white workers is accepted since the probability of obtaining this result by chance is high (that is, $p = 0.90$). In other words, since there is no significant difference between the obtained and the hypothesised result, we would conclude that there are equal numbers of white and non-white workers.

Incidentally, the similarity of these examples to those used to illustrate the notion of significance testing in the previous chapter should be noted, except that there we were comparing the frequency of finding one tail (or one male) to every five heads (or five females) against an expected frequency or probability of 0.5. To work this out using SPSS, we would have to create a data file which consisted of one sequence of such a frequency and then carry out a binomial test on it.

Chi-square test for one sample

If we want to compare the observed frequencies of cases with those expected in a variable which has more than two categories, then we use a chi-square or χ^2 (pronounced 'kye-square') test rather than a binomial test. If, for instance, we wished to know whether there were equal numbers of workers from the four different ethnic groups coded in our Job Survey data, then we would use a chi-square test for one sample. We would use the following procedure to do this:

→**Analyze** →**Nonparametric Tests** →**Chi-Square…** [opens **Chi-Square Test** dialog box shown in Box 7.2]

Box 7.2 **Chi-Square Test** dialog box

→**ethnicgp** →▶button [puts **ethnicgp** under **Test Variable List:**] →**Use specified range** and type **1** [in box labelled **Lower:**] →box called **Upper:** and type **4** →**OK**

The range of categories to be examined needs to be specified if not all of them are to be included. In this example, we have chosen to exclude the 'other' category by listing categories one to four. This fifth category would have been included in this analysis by default if we had not specifically excluded it.

The expected frequencies are assumed to be equal, unless explicitly specified otherwise. In other words, in this case we are testing the hypothesis that the four categories will contain the same number of workers, or one in four. If we expect them to be different, then we need to list these expected frequencies. If, for example, we know that in the industry covered by our Job Survey the ratio of workers in these four categories is 95:2:2:1 and we wish to find out if our sample is similar to the population in this respect, we would do this by specifying these expected frequencies by selecting **Values:** (in the section labelled **Expected Values**), typing the first value in the adjoining box, selecting **Add** and repeating this sequence for the other three expected frequencies before selecting **OK**. Expected frequencies need to be greater than zero and are specified as a proportion of those listed. In this case, 95 out of 100 are expected to be white since the total adds up to 100 (95+2+2+1).

The output for the first procedure is shown in Table 7.4. Note that for this test the display includes the numbers of the categories, the number of cases observed and expected in each of these categories, the residual or difference between the

Table 7.4 One-sample chi-square test comparing number of
people in ethnic groups (Job Survey)

Frequencies

	Category	ETHNIC GP		
		Observed N	Expected N	Residual
1	White	36	17.5	18.5
2	Asian	18	17.5	.5
3	West Indian	14	17.5	-3.5
4	African	2	17.5	-15.5
Total		70		

Test Statistics

	ETHNICGP
Chi-Square[a]	.000
df	3
Asymp. Sig.	.000

a. 0 cells (.0%) have expected frequencies less than
5. The minimum expected cell frequency is 17.5.

observed and the expected frequencies, the chi-square statistic, the degrees of freedom and the level of significance.

The term *degrees of freedom (d.f.)*, associated with any statistic, refers to the number of components which are free to vary. It is a difficult concept which is well explained elsewhere (Walker, 1940). In this case, they are calculated by subtracting 1 from the number of categories. Since there are four categories, there are three degrees of freedom (that is, 4−1). What this means essentially is that if we know the size of the sample and if we know the observed frequencies in three of the four categories, then we can work out from this the observed frequencies in the remaining category. In other words, if we know one of the values, the other three are free to vary.

As we can see, the observed frequencies are significantly different ($p<0.0005$) from the expected ones of there being an equal number of cases in each of the four categories. In other words, since the probability of obtaining this result by chance is very low (at least 5 out of 10,000 times), we would conclude that the number of workers in each ethnic group is not equal.

There is a restriction on using chi-square when the expected frequencies are small. With only two categories (or one degree of freedom), the number of cases expected to fall in these categories should be at least five before this test can be applied. If the expected frequencies are less than five, then the binomial test should be used instead. With three or more categories (or more than one degree of freedom), chi-square should not be used when any expected frequency is smaller than one or when more than 20 per cent of the expected frequencies are smaller than five. In these situations, it may be possible to increase the expected frequencies in a category by combining it with those of another.

Table 7.5 One-sample chi-square with insufficient cases
(Job Survey)

Frequencies

	Category	Observed N	Expected N	Residual
		ETHNICGP		
1	White	36	66.5	-30.5
2	Asian	18	1.4	16.6
3	West Indian	14	1.4	12.6
4	African	2	.7	1.3
Total		70		

Test Statistics

	ETHNICGP
Chi-Square[a]	.000
df	3
Asymp. Sig.	.000

a. 3 cells (75.0%) have expected frequencies less than 5. The minimum expected cell frequency is .7.

An example of the latter case is the second statistical analysis we asked for, the output of which is presented in Table 7.5. Here, three of the expected frequencies fall below 2, one of which is below 1. We would need a much larger sample of participants to use a chi-square test on these data. If we had only two categories, whites and non-whites, we would require a minimum sample of 100 in order to have an expected frequency of 5 in the non-white category. Consequently, it would be necessary to use a binomial test to determine if the frequency of non-whites in the Job Survey is different from a hypothesised one of 5 per cent.

Chi-square test for two or more unrelated samples

If we wanted to compare the frequency of cases found in one variable in two or more unrelated samples or categories of another variable, we would also use the chi-square test. We shall illustrate this test with the relatively simple example in which we have two dichotomous variables, gender (male and female) and ethnic group (white and non-white), although it can also be applied to two variables which have three or more categories. Suppose, for instance, we wished to find out whether the proportion of male to female workers was the same in both white and black workers.

First of all, we have to recode the category of ethnic group, so that all the non-whites are coded as 2. If we wanted to assign value labels, we would have to provide new ones for the two groups. Second, because the chi-square test for two or more unrelated samples is only available as part of the SPSS procedure for generating tables which show the distribution of two or more variables, we have to use the relevant options in this **Crosstabs** procedure. Further details on it can be found in the next chapter, where its operation is described more fully. In order not to replicate this information, only the basic steps for generating chi-square will be outlined here, which for this analysis are as follows:

→**Analyze** →**Descriptive Statistics** →**Crosstabs...** [opens **Crosstabs** dialog box shown in Box 7.3]
→**gender** →▶button [puts **gender** under **Row[s]:**] →**ethncgpc** →▶button [puts **ethncgpc** under **Column[s]:**] →**Cells...** [opens **Crosstabs: Cell Display** sub-dialog box shown in Box 7.4]
→**Expected** [in **Counts** section] →**Unstandardized** [in **Residuals** section]
→**Continue** [closes **Crosstabs: Cell Display** subdialog box]
→**Statistics...** [opens **Crosstabs: Statistics** subdialog box shown in Box 7.5]
→**Chi-square** →**Continue** [closes **Crosstabs: Statistics** subdialog box]
→**OK**

Since chi-square is based on comparing the expected with the observed frequency in each cell, it is useful to have a display of the expected frequencies and the difference (the unstandardised residual) between the expected and the observed frequencies.

Box 7.3 **Crosstabs** dialog box

Box 7.4 **Crosstabs: Cell Display** subdialog box

Box 7.5 **Crosstabs: Statistics** subdialog box

The output from this procedure is shown in Table 7.6 which includes a table of the expected and observed frequencies in each cell, their difference, the Pearson chi-square statistic, the degrees of freedom, the significance level and the minimum expected frequency. This last value is useful when the degrees of freedom are

Table 7.6 Chi-square test produced by **Crosstabs** comparing number of white and non-white men and women

GENDER * ETHNCGPC Crosstabulation

			ETHNCGPC		Total
			White	Non-white	
GENDER	Men	Count	22	17	39
		Expected Count	20.1	18.9	39.0
		Residual	1.9	-1.9	
	Women	Count	14	17	31
		Expected Count	15.9	15.1	31.0
		Residual	-1.9	1.9	
Total		Count	36	34	70
		Expected Count	36.0	34.0	70.0

Chi-Square Tests

	Value	df	Asymp. Sig. (2-sided)	Exact Sig. (2-sided)	Exact Sig. (1-sided)
Pearson Chi-Square	.875[b]	1	.350		
Continuity Correction[a]	.483	1	.487		
Likelihood Ratio	.876	1	.349		
Fisher's Exact Test				.471	.244
Linear-by-Linear Association	.862	1	.353		
N of Valid Cases	70				

a. Computed only for a 2x2 table

b. 0 cells (.0%) have expected count less than 5. The minimum expected count is 15.06.

larger than one, because as in the case of a one-sample chi-square, this test should not be used if any cell has an expected frequency of less than 1 or if 20 per cent or more of the cells have an expected frequency of less than 5. As the minimum expected frequency in any one cell is 15.1 (for non-white females) and there are no cells with an expected frequency of less than 5, it is appropriate to use this test. The degrees of freedom are calculated by subtracting 1 from the number of categories in each of the two variables and multiplying the remaining values (that is, $(2-1)$ $(2-1)=1$). The observed frequencies are displayed above the expected ones in each of the cells. Thus, the observed frequency of white males is 22, while the expected one is 20.1. The residual or difference is 1.9. Two chi-squares are given. The first chi-square is the uncorrected value while the second incorporates Yates's correction which assumes that the frequencies can be non-integral (that is, consist of whole numbers and fractions or decimals). Yates's correction is only given for 2×2 tables and may no longer be needed (Cramer, 1998). Since the value of chi-square is not significant, this means that the proportion of male to female workers is the same for both whites and non-whites.

McNemar test for two related samples

This test is used to compare the frequencies of a dichotomous variable from the same cases at two points in time, in two treatments, or from two samples which have been matched to be similar in certain respects such as having the same distributions of age, gender and socio-economic status. Suppose, for example, we wanted to find out if there had been any changes in the attendance of workers at a firm's monthly meetings in two consecutive months (**attend1** and **attend2**). The use of tests to analyse information from two or more related samples is illustrated with the small set of data in Table 7.7. This consists of one example of the three kinds of variables (categorical, ordinal and interval/ratio) measured at three consecutive monthly intervals on twelve workers. The categorical variable is their attendance at the firm's monthly meeting (**attend1** to **attend3**), the ordinal one is the quality of their work as rated by their supervisor (**qual1** to **qual3**), while the interval/ratio one is their self-expressed job satisfaction (**satis1** to **satis3**). A study in which data are collected from the same individuals at two or more points is known as a *prospective*, *longitudinal* or *panel* design. Consequently, this example will be referred to as the Panel Study.

To conduct a McNemar test comparing **attend1** and **attend2** we use the following SPSS procedure:

→**A**nalyze →**N**onparametric Tests →**2 Related Samples…** [opens **Two-Related-Samples Tests** dialog box shown in Box 7.6]
→**attend1** [puts **attend1** beside **Variable 1:** in **Current Selections** section]
→**attend2** [puts **attend2** beside **Variable 2:** in **Current Selections** section]
→▶button [puts the **attend1** and **attend2** under **Test Pair[s] List:**] →**W**ilcoxon [to de-select] →**M**c**N**emar →**OK**

The output for this procedure is presented in Table 7.8. The table shows the number of people whose attendance changed or remained the same from the first

Table 7.7 The Panel Study data

Id	Attend1	Qual1	Satis1	Attend2	Qual2	Satis2	Attend3	Qual3	Satis3
01	1	5	17	1	4	18	1	5	16
02	1	4	12	2	3	9	2	2	7
03	2	3	13	1	4	15	2	3	14
04	2	4	11	2	5	14	2	3	8
05	2	2	7	2	3	10	1	3	9
06	1	4	14	1	4	15	2	3	10
07	1	3	15	2	1	6	1	4	12
08	2	4	12	1	3	9	1	4	13
09	1	4	13	2	5	14	1	3	15
10	1	1	5	2	2	4	2	3	9
11	1	3	8	2	3	7	1	3	6
12	1	4	11	2	4	13	1	3	10

Two-Related-Samples Tests

Variables list:
- attend1
- qual1
- satis1
- attend2
- qual2
- satis2
- attend3
- qual3

Test Pair(s) List:
attend1 -- attend2

Buttons: OK, Paste, Reset, Cancel, Help

Current Selections
Variable 1:
Variable 2:

Test Type
☐ Wilcoxon ☐ Sign ☑ McNemar
☐ Marginal Homogeneity

Exact... Options...

Box 7.6 **Two-Related-Samples Tests** dialog box

Table 7.8 McNemar test comparing attendance across two months (Panel Study)

ATTEND1 & ATTEND2

	ATTEND2	
ATTEND1	1	2
1	2	6
2	2	2

Test Statistics[b]

	ATTEND1 & ATTEND2
N	12
Exact Sig.(2-tailed)	.289[a]

a. Binomial distribution used.

b. McNemar Test

to the second month. Since attendance is coded as 1 and non-attendance as 2, we can see that six workers attended the first but not the second meeting and that two attended the second but not the first one. If fewer than twenty-six cases change from one sample to another, as they did here, the binomial test is computed. Otherwise, the one-sample chi-square test is used. As the two-tailed level of probability is greater than 0.05, this means that there was no significant change in attendance between the first and second meeting. In other words, we would conclude that a similar number of people attended the first and the second meeting.

Cochran Q test for three or more related samples

To compare the distribution of a dichotomous variable across three or more related samples, the Cochran Q test is applied. Thus, we would use the following procedure to compute this test if we wanted to examine attendance at the firm's meeting over the three month period in the Panel Study:

→**Analyze** →**Nonparametric Tests** →**K Related Samples…** [opens **Tests for Several Related Samples** dialog box shown in Box 7.7]
→**attend1** →▶button [puts **attend1** under **Test Variables:**] →**attend2** →
▶button [puts **attend2** under **Test Variables:**] →**attend3** →▶button [puts **attend3** under **Test Variables:**] →**Friedman** [to de-select] →**Cochran's Q** →**OK**

This procedure produced the output in Table 7.9. This shows the number of people who did and did not attend the three meetings. Once again, as the probability level is above 0.05, this indicates there is no significant difference in attendance over the three meetings.

NON-CATEGORICAL VARIABLES AND NON-PARAMETRIC TESTS

Kolmogorov–Smirnov test for one sample

This test is used to compare the observed frequencies of the values of an ordinal variable, such as rated quality of work, against some specified theoretical distribution. It determines the statistical significance of the largest difference between them. In SPSS, the theoretical distribution can be **Normal**, **Uniform**, **Poisson** or

Box 7.7 **Tests for Several Related Samples** dialog box

Table 7.9 Cochran *Q* test comparing attendance across three months (Panel Study)

Frequencies

	Value	
	1	2
ATTEND1	8	4
ATTEND2	4	8
ATTEND3	7	5

Test Statistics

N	12
Cochran's Q	2.600[a]
df	2
Asymp. Sig.	.273

a. 1 is treated as a success.

Exponential. These are the keywords which must be used to specify which one of these three options is to be selected. Thus, for example, if we expected the five degrees of rated quality of work (that is, very poor, poor, average, good, and very good) in the Job Survey to appear equally often (that is, as a uniform distribution), we would use the following procedure:

→**Analyze** →**Nonparametric Tests** →**1-Sample K-S...** [opens **One-Sample Kolmogorov-Smirnov Test** dialog box shown in Box 7.8]
→**qual** →▶button [puts **qual** under **Test Variable List:**] →**Normal** [to deselect] →**Uniform** [under **Test Distribution**] →**OK**

Box 7.8 **One-Sample Kolmogorov-Smirnov Test** dialog box

Table 7.10 One-sample Kolmogorov–Smirnov test
          comparing distribution of quality of
          work (Job Survey)

One-Sample Kolmogorov-Smirnov Test 2

		QUAL
N		70
Uniform Parameters[a,b]	Minimum	1
	Maximum	5
Most Extreme	Absolute	.207
Differences	Positive	.129
	Negative	-.207
Kolmogorov-Smirnov Z		1.733
Asymp. Sig. (2-tailed)		.005

a. Test distribution is Uniform.
b. Calculated from data.

The lowest and the highest values in the sample data will be used. In other words, if the lowest rating is 2 and the highest 4, then SPSS will compare the distribution of this range of values. The sample mean and standard deviation are used for the normal distribution and the sample mean for the Poisson distribution.

The second table in the output from this procedure is displayed in Table 7.10. The largest absolute, positive and negative differences between the observed and theoretical distributions are printed, together with the Kolmogorov–Smirnov Z statistic and its probability value. The largest absolute difference is simply the largest difference, regardless of its direction. Since p is well below the two-tailed 0.05 level, the difference is significant. This means the number of cases at each of the five levels is not equal.

Kolmogorov–Smirnov test for two unrelated samples

This test is also used to compare the distribution of values in two groups. Thus, for example, the following procedure is used to see if the distribution of the ratings of quality of work among men is different from that among women:

→**Analyze** →**Nonparametric Tests** →**2 Independent Samples...** [opens **Two-Independent-Samples Tests** dialog box shown in Box 7.9]
→**qual** →▶button [puts **qual** under **Test Variable List:**] →**gender** [puts **gender** under **Grouping Variable:**] →**Define Groups...** [opens **Two Independent Samples: Define Groups** subdialog box shown in Box 7.10]
→in box beside **Group 1:** type 1 →box beside **Group 2:** and type 2 →**Continue** [closes **Two Independent Samples: Define Groups** subdialog box]
→**Mann-Whitney U** [to de-select] →**Kolmogorov-Smirnov Z** →**OK**

Box 7.9 **Two-Independent-Samples Tests** dialog box

Box 7.10 **Two Independent Samples: Define Groups** subdialog box

This procedure produced the output in Table 7.11. Once again, the largest absolute, positive and negative differences are shown, together with the Z statistic. The number of cases or participants in each of the two groups being compared is also shown. As p is well above the two-tailed 0.05 level, this means there is no difference in the distribution of quality of work ratings for men and women.

Median test for two or more unrelated samples

The median test is used to determine if the distribution of values either side of a common median differs for two or more unrelated samples. If we want to determine if the distribution of rated quality of work is similar for men and women, we would use the following procedure:

Table 7.11 Two-sample Kolmogorov–Smirnov test comparing distribution of quality of work in men and women (Job Survey)

Frequencies

	GENDER	N
QUAL	Men	39
	Women	31
	Total	70

Test Statistics[a]

		QUAL
Most Extreme	Absolute	.126
Differences	Positive	.017
	Negative	-.126
Kolmogorov-Smirnov Z		.522
Asymp. Sig. (2-tailed)		.948

a. Grouping Variable: GENDER

➜**Analyze** ➜**Nonparametric Tests** ➜**K Independent Samples…** [opens **Tests for Several Independent Samples** dialog box shown in Box 7.11]
➜**qual** ➜▶button [puts **qual** under **Test Variable List:**] ➜**gender** [puts **gender** under **Grouping Variable:**] ➜**Define Range…** [opens a **Define Range** subdialog box like that shown in Box 7.12]
➜in box beside **Minimum:** type **1** ➜box beside **Maximum:** and type **2** ➜**Continue** [closes **Several Independent Samples: Define Range** subdialog box]
➜**Kruskal-Wallis H** [to de-select] ➜**Median** ➜**OK**

Box 7.11 **Tests for Several Independent Samples** dialog box

```
┌─────────────────────────────────────────────────────┐
│ Several Independent Samples: Define Range  [X]       │
├─────────────────────────────────────────────────────┤
│  Range for Grouping Variable        ┌──────────┐     │
│                                     │ Continue │     │
│  Mjnimum:       │1 │                └──────────┘     │
│                                     ┌──────────┐     │
│  Maximum:       │2 │                │  Cancel  │     │
│                                     └──────────┘     │
│                                     ┌──────────┐     │
│                                     │   Help   │     │
│                                     └──────────┘     │
└─────────────────────────────────────────────────────┘
```

Box 7.12 **Several Independent Samples: Define Range** subdialog box

Table 7.12 Median test comparing quality of work
in men and women (Job Survey)

Frequencies

		GENDER	
		Men	Women
QUAL	> Median	20	12
	<= Median	19	19

Test Statistics[a]

		QUAL
N		70
Median		3.00
Chi-Square		1.100
df		1
Asymp. Sig.		.294
Yates' Continuity	Chi-Square	.652
Correction	df	1
	Asymp. Sig.	.419

a. Grouping Variable: GENDER

This procedure gave the output in Table 7.12. It has a 2×2 table showing the number of cases above the median and less than or equal to it for males and females. We can see that there are twenty men above the median and nineteen below or equal to it. Also given is the median value which is 3, the chi-square statistic (uncorrected and corrected for continuity) and its significance. Because p is greater than 0.05 (for both values) and therefore not significant, the median rating of work quality does not differ for men and women.

Mann–Whitney *U* test for two unrelated samples

The Mann–Whitney test is more powerful than the median test because it compares the number of times a score from one of the samples is ranked higher than a score from the other sample rather than the number of scores which are above the

Table 7.13 Mann–Whitney test comparing quality of work in men and women (Job Survey)

Ranks

GENDER		N	Mean Rank	Sum of Ranks
QUAL	Men	39	36.94	1440.50
	Women	31	33.69	1044.50
	Total	70		

Test Statistics^a

	QUAL
Mann-Whitney U	548.500
Wilcoxon W	1044.500
Z	-.680
Asymp. Sig. (2-tailed)	.496

a. Grouping Variable: GENDER

median. If the two groups are similar, then the number of times this happens should also be similar for the two groups. The procedure for comparing the rated quality of work for men and women is:

→**Analyze** →**Nonparametric Tests** →**2 Independent Samples…** [opens **Two-Independent-Samples Tests** dialog box shown in Box 7.9]
→**qual** →▶button [puts **qual** under **Test Variable List:**] →**gender** [puts **gender** under **Grouping Variable:**] →**Define Groups…** [opens **Two Independent Samples: Define Groups** subdialog box shown in Box 7.10]
→in box beside **Group 1:** type **1** →box beside **Group 2:** and type **2** →**Continue** [closes **Two Independent Samples: Define Groups** subdialog box]
[→**Mann-Whitney U** already selected] →**OK**

The output produced by this procedure is shown in Table 7.13. It gives the mean rank of the ratings for men and women, the number of cases on which these are based, the Mann–Whitney *U* statistic, and the Wilcoxon *W* (which is the sum of the ranks of the smaller group and which we can ignore). Since it is necessary to correct for the number of scores which receive, or tie for, the same rank, it does this by giving the *Z* statistic and its significance level. Although the significance of *U* is not shown here, correcting for ties increases the value of *Z* slightly. As the *Z* statistic is still not significant (that is, *p* is greater than 0.05), there is no difference between men and women in the mean ranking of the rated quality of their work.

Kruskal–Wallis *H* test for three or more unrelated samples

The Kruskal–Wallis *H* test is similar to the Mann–Whitney *U* test in that the cases in the different samples are ranked together in one series. However, unlike the

Table 7.14 Kruskal–Wallis test comparing quality of
work between ethnic groups (Job Survey)

Ranks

	ETHNICGP	N	Mean Rank
QUAL	White	36	34.99
	Asian	18	33.47
	West Indian	14	37.71
	African	2	47.50
	Total	70	

Test Statistics[a,b]

	QUAL
Chi-Square	1.121
df	3
Asymp. Sig.	.772

a. Kruskal-Wallis Test

b. Grouping Variable: ETHNICGP

Mann–Whitney U test, it can be used to compare scores in more than two groups. To compare the rated quality of work for people in the four ethnic groups, we use the following procedure:

→**Analyze** →**Nonparametric Tests** →**K Independent Samples...** [opens **Tests for Several Independent Samples** dialog box shown in Box 7.11]
→**qual** →▸button [puts **qual** under **Test Variable List:**] →**ethnicgp** [puts **ethnicgp** under **Grouping Variable:**] →**Define Range...** [opens a **Define Range** subdialog box like that shown in Box 7.12]
→in box beside **Minimum:** type **1** →box beside **Maximum:** and type **4**
→**Continue** [closes **Several Independent Samples: Define Range** subdialog box]
→**Kruskal-Wallis** →**OK**

This procedure produced the output in Table 7.14. It shows the mean rank for each group, the number of cases in them, and the chi-square statistic and its significance level corrected for rank ties. Since the significance level is greater than 0.05, this indicates there is no difference between workers of the four ethnic groups in the mean ranking of the rated quality of their work.

Sign test for two related samples

The sign test compares the number of positive and negative differences between two scores from the same or similar (that is, matched) samples such as those in the Panel Study, and ignores the size of these differences. If the two samples are similar, then these differences should be normally distributed. Thus, for example, we could compare the rated quality of work at two of the times (say, **qual1** and **qual2**) in the Panel Study. If the number of positive differences (that is, decreases in ratings) was similar to the number of negative ones (that is, increases in ratings), this would mean that there was no change in one particular direction between the two occasions. To compute this comparison, we use the following procedure:

→**Analyze** →**Nonparametric Tests** →**2 Related Samples…** [opens **Two-Related-Samples Tests** dialog box shown in Box 7.6]
→**qual1** [puts **qual1** beside **Variable 1:** in **Current Selections** section]
→**qual2** [puts **qual2** beside **Variable 2:** in **Current Selections** section] →
▶button [puts **qual1** and **qual2** under **Test Pair[s] List:**] →**Wilcoxon** [to de-select] →**Sign** →**OK**

This procedure produced the output in Table 7.15. It displays the number of negative, positive and zero (ties) differences. There are three ties, five positive differences and four negative ones. Since fewer than twenty-six differences were found, it gives the binomial significance level. If more than twenty-five differences had been obtained, it would have given the significance level for the Z statistic. With almost equal numbers of positive and negative differences, it is not surprising that the test is non-significant. In other words, there is no change in rated quality of work over the two months.

Table 7.15 Sign test comparing quality across two months (Panel Study)

Frequencies

		N
QUAL2 - QUAL1	Negative Differences[a]	4
	Positive Differences[b]	5
	Ties[c]	3
	Total	12

a. QUAL2 < QUAL1
b. QUAL2 > QUAL1
c. QUAL1 = QUAL2

Test Statistics[b]

	QUAL2 - QUAL1
Exact Sig. (2-tailed)	1.000[a]

a. Binomial distribution used.
b. Sign Test

Wilcoxon matched-pairs signed-ranks test for two related samples

This test, like the Mann–Whitney, takes account of the size of the differences between two sets of related scores by ranking and then summing those with the same sign. If there are no differences between the two samples, then the number of positive signs should be similar to that of the negative ones. This test would be used, for example, to determine if the rated quality of work in the Panel Study was the same in the first and second month (**qual1** and **qual2**). To do this we would use the following procedure:

→**Analyze** →**Nonparametric Tests** →**2 Related Samples…** [opens **Two-Related-Samples Tests** dialog box shown in Box 7.6]
→**qual1** [puts **qual1** beside **Variable 1:** in **Current Selections** section]
→**qual2** [puts **qual2** beside **Variable 2:** in **Current Selections** section] →
▶button [puts **qual1** and **qual2** under **Test Pair[s] List:**] →**Wilcoxon** →**OK**

Table 7.16 contains the output for this procedure. It presents the mean rank and sum of ranks for the negative and positive ranks, the number of cases on which these are based together with the number of tied ranks, the test statistic Z, and its significance level. We obtain the same result with this test. The mean rank of rated quality of work does not differ between the two months.

Table 7.16 Wilcoxon matched-pairs signed-ranks test comparing job quality across first two months (Panel Study)

Ranks

		N	Mean Rank	Sum of Ranks
QUAL2 - QUAL1	Negative Ranks	4[a]	5.63	22.50
	Positive Ranks	5[b]	4.50	22.50
	Ties	3[c]		
	Total	12		

a. QUAL2 < QUAL1
b. QUAL2 > QUAL1
c. QUAL1 = QUAL2

Test Statistics[b]

	QUAL2 - QUAL1
Z	.000[a]
Asymp. Sig. (2-tailed)	1.000

a. The sum of negative ranks equals the sum of positive ranks.
b. Wilcoxon Signed Ranks Test

Friedman test for three or more related samples

If we wanted to compare the scores of three or more related samples, such as the rated quality of work across all three months rather than just two of them, we would use the Friedman two-way analysis of variance test. It ranks the scores for each of the cases and then calculates the mean rank score for each sample. If there are no differences between the samples, their mean ranks should be similar. We would use the following procedure to compare the quality of work over the three months in the Panel Study:

→**Analyze** →**Nonparametric Tests** →**K Related Samples...** [opens **Tests for Several Related Samples** dialog box shown in Box 7.7]
→**qual1** →▶button [puts **qual1** under **Test Variables:**] →**qual2** →▶button [puts **qual2** under **Test Variables:**] →**qual3** →▶button [puts **qual3** under **Test Variables:**] →**Friedman** →**OK**

The output produced by this procedure is shown in Table 7.17. It contains the mean rank for the three samples, the number of cases in them, the chi-square statistic, its degrees of freedom (which is the number of samples minus 1) and its significance level. The non-significant chi-square means there is no difference in the mean ranks of rated quality of work across the three months.

NON-CATEGORICAL VARIABLES AND PARAMETRIC TESTS

t test for one sample

This test is used to determine if the mean of a sample is similar to that of the population. If, for example, we know that the mean score for job satisfaction for workers in the industry covered in the Job Survey is 10 and we want to find out if the mean of our sample is similar to it, we would carry out a *t* test. To do this with SPSS, we carry out the following procedure.

→**Analyze** →**Compare Means** →**One-Sample T Test...**
[opens **One-Sample T Test** dialog box shown in Box 7.13]
→**satis** →▶button [puts **satis** under **Test Variable[s]:**] →type **10** in box beside **Test Value:** →**OK**

The output for this procedure is shown in Table 7.18. We see that there is a significant difference between the population mean of 10 and the sample mean of 10.84 at the two-tailed probability level of 0.04.

Table 7.17 Friedman test comparing job quality across three months (Panel Study)

Ranks

	Mean Rank
QUAL1	2.04
QUAL2	2.13
QUAL3	1.83

Test Statistics[a]

N	12
Chi-Square	.684
df	2
Asymp. Sig.	.710

a. Friedman Test

Box 7.13 **One-Sample T Test** dialog box

Table 7.18 One-sample *t* test for job satisfaction (Job Survey)

One-Sample Statistics

	N	Mean	Std. Deviation	Std. Error Mean
SATIS	68	10.8382	3.3036	.4006

One-Sample Test

	Test Value = 10					
					95% Confidence Interval of the Difference	
	t	df	Sig. (2-tailed)	Mean Difference	Lower	Upper
SATIS	2.092	67	.040	.8382	3.859E-02	1.6379

Standard error of the mean

It is necessary to outline more fully what the *standard error of the mean* is, since this important idea also constitutes the basis of other parametric tests such as the analysis of variance. One of the assumptions of many parametric tests is that the population of the variable to be analysed should be normally distributed. The errors of most distributions are known to take this form. For example, if a large group of people were asked to guess today's temperature, the distribution of their guesses would approximate that of a normal distribution, even if the temperature does not itself represent a normal distribution. In addition, it has been observed that the distribution of certain characteristics also takes this form. If, for example, you plot the distribution of the heights of a large group of adult human beings, it will be similar to that of a normal distribution.

If we draw samples from a population of values which is normally distributed, then the means of those samples will also be normally distributed. In other words, most of the means will be very similar to that of the population, although some of them will vary quite considerably. The standard error of the mean represents the standard deviation of the sample means. The one-sample *t* test compares the mean of a sample with that of the population in terms of how likely it is that that difference has arisen by chance. The smaller this difference is, the more likely it is to have resulted from chance.

t test for two unrelated means

This test is used to determine if the means of two unrelated samples differ. It does this by comparing the difference between the two means with the standard error of the difference in the means of different samples:

$$t = \frac{\text{sample one mean} - \text{sample two mean}}{\text{standard error of the difference in means}}$$

The *standard error of the difference in means*, like the standard error of the mean, is also normally distributed. If we draw a large number of samples from a population whose values are normally distributed and plot the differences in the means of each of these samples, the shape of this distribution will be normal. Since the means of most of the samples will be close to the mean of the population and therefore similar to one another, if we subtract them from each other the differences between them will be close to zero. In other words, the nearer the difference in the means of two samples is to zero, the more likely it is that this difference is due to chance.

To compare the means of two samples, such as the mean job satisfaction of male and female workers in the Job Survey, we would use the following procedure:

→**Analyze** →**Compare Means** →**Independent-Samples T Test...** [opens **Independent-Samples T Test** dialog box shown in Box 7.14]
→**satis** →▶button [puts **satis** under **Test Variable[s]:**] →**gender** [puts **gender**

Box 7.14 **Independent-Samples T Test** dialog box

Box 7.15 **Define Groups** subdialog box

under **Grouping Variable:**] →**Define Groups...** [opens **Define Groups** subdialog box shown in Box 7.15]
→in box beside **Group 1:** type **1** →box beside **Group 2:** and type **2** →**Continue**
[closes **Define Groups** subdialog box]
→**OK**

There are two ways of defining the two groups. First, we can define them in terms
of their two codes (**1** and **2**), as has been done above. Second, one of the values can
be used as a cut-off point, at or above which all the values constitute one group
while those below form the other group. In this instance, the cut-off point is 2,
which would be placed in parentheses after gender.

The output for this procedure is displayed in Table 7.19. The number of cases in
the two groups, together with their means, standard deviations and standard errors,

Table 7.19 Unrelated *t* test comparing job satisfaction in men and women
(Job Survey)

Group Statistics

	GENDER	N	Mean	Std. Deviation	Std. Error Mean
SATIS	Men	37	10.9459	3.3245	.5466
	Women	31	10.7097	3.3286	.5978

Independent Samples Test

		Levene's Test for Equality of Variances		t-test for Equality of Means						
									95% Confidence Interval of the Difference	
		F	Sig.	t	df	Sig. (2-tailed)	Mean Difference	Std. Error Difference	Lower	Upper
SATIS	Equal variances assumed	.117	.733	.292	66	.771	.2363	.8099	-1.3808	1.8533
	Equal variances not assumed			.292	63.904	.771	.2363	.8100	-1.3820	1.8545

is listed. Since we do not know what the standard error of the difference in means is of the population in question, we have to estimate it. How this is done depends on whether the difference in the variances of the two samples is statistically significant. This information is provided by the Levene's test for equality of variances. Levene's test is a one-way analysis of variance on the absolute (that is, ignoring the minus sign) deviation scores of the groups where the group mean is subtracted from each of the individual scores within that group. A one-way analysis of variance for three or more groups is described below. In this case the one-way analysis would be done on only two groups. If Levene's test is significant (that is, has a probability of 0.05 or less), then the variances are unequal and so the *separate* variance estimate is used to calculate the *t* value. If the variances are equal, the *pooled* variance estimate is employed for this purpose. In Table 7.19, the variances are not statistically different since the *p* value of Levene's test is 0.733. Consequently, we look at the *t* value based on equal variances. This is non-significant with a two-tailed *p* value of 0.771. In other words, we would conclude that there is no significant difference in mean job satisfaction between males and females. The two-tailed test of significance is provided by default. To calculate the one-tailed level of significance, divide the two-tailed one by 2, which in this case would still be non-significant at 0.386 (0.771/2).

It should be pointed out that the variance, the standard deviation and the standard error of a sample are related. The *variance* or mean squared deviation is calculated by subtracting the mean of the sample from each of its scores (to provide a measure of their deviation from the mean), squaring them, adding them together and dividing them by one less than the number of cases. Since the deviations would sum to zero, they are squared to make the negative deviations positive. The *standard deviation* is simply the square root of the variance. The advantage of the standard deviation over the variance is that it is expressed in the original values of the data. For example, the standard deviation of job satisfaction is described in terms of the twenty points on this scale. The *standard error* is the standard deviation divided by the square root of the number of cases. The relationships between these three measures can be checked out on the statistics shown in Table 7.19.

Unrelated *t* test and ordinal data

Some people have argued that parametric tests should only be used on interval/ratio data (for example, Stevens, 1946). Others, as we have mentioned earlier, have reasoned that such a restriction is unnecessary. In view of this controversy, it may be interesting to see whether the use of an unrelated *t* test on an ordinal variable such as rated quality of work gives very dissimilar results to that of the Mann–Whitney test previously used. According to Siegel and Castellan (1988), the Mann–Whitney test is about 95 per cent as powerful as the *t* test. What this means is that the *t* test requires 5 per cent fewer participants than the Mann–Whitney test to reject the null hypothesis when it is false. The following procedure was used to generate the output in Table 7.20:

→**Analyze** →**Compare** **Means** →**Independent-Samples** **T** **Test...** [opens **Independent-Samples T Test** dialog box shown in Box 7.14]
→**qual** →▶button [puts **qual** under **Test Variable[s]:**] →**gender** [puts **gender** under **Grouping Variable:**] →**Define Groups...** [opens **Define Groups** sub-dialog box shown in Box 7.15]
→in box beside **Group 1:** type 1 →box beside **Group 2:** and type 2 →**Continue** [closes **Define Groups** subdialog box]
→**OK**

As can be seen, this test also indicates that there is no significant difference between men and women in the mean of their rated quality of work.

Table 7.20 *t* test comparing quality of work in men and women (Job Survey)

Group Statistics

	GENDER	N	Mean	Std. Deviation	Std. Error Mean
QUAL	Men	39	3.28	1.21	.19
	Women	31	3.06	1.34	.24

Independent Samples Test

		Levene's Test for Equality of Variances		t-test for Equality of Means						
									95% Confidence Interval of the Difference	
		F	Sig.	t	df	Sig. (2-tailed)	Mean Difference	Std. Error Difference	Lower	Upper
QUAL	Equal variances assumed	.000	.987	.712	68	.479	.22	.31	-.39	.83
	Equal variances not assumed			.703	61.277	.484	.22	.31	-.40	.84

ONE-WAY ANALYSIS OF VARIANCE FOR THREE OR MORE UNRELATED MEANS

To compare the means of three or more unrelated samples, such as the mean job satisfaction of the four ethnic groups in the Job Survey, it is necessary to compute a one-way analysis of variance. This is essentially an *F* test in which an estimate of the *between-groups* variance (or *mean-square* as the estimate of the variance is referred to in analysis of variance) is compared with an estimate of the *within-groups* variance by dividing the former by the latter:

$$F = \frac{\text{between-groups estimated variance or mean-square}}{\text{within-groups estimated variance or mean-square}}$$

The total amount of variance in the dependent variable (that is, job satisfaction) can be thought of as comprising two elements: that which is due to the independent variable (that is, ethnic group) and that which is due to other factors. This latter component is often referred to as *error* or *residual* variance. The variance that is due to the independent variable is frequently described as *explained* variance. If the between-groups (that is, explained) estimated variance is considerably larger than that within-groups (that is, error or residual), then the value of the *F* ratio will be higher, which implies that the differences between the means are unlikely to be due to chance.

The within-groups mean-square or estimated variance is its sum-of-squares divided by its degrees of freedom. These degrees of freedom are the sum of the number of cases minus one in each group (that is, [the number of cases in group one -1]+[the number of cases in group two -1] and so on). The sum-of-squares is the sum of squared differences between each score in a group and its mean, summed across all groups. The between-groups sum-of-squares, on the other hand, is obtained by subtracting each group's mean from the overall (total or grand) mean, squaring them, multiplying them by the number of cases in each group, and summing the result. It can also be calculated by subtracting the within-groups sum-of-squares from the total sum-of-squares since the total sum-of-squares is the sum of the between- and within-groups sum-of-squares:

$$\begin{array}{c} \text{total} \\ \text{sum-of-squares} \end{array} = \begin{array}{c} \text{between-groups} \\ \text{sum-of-squares} \\ \text{(i.e. explained)} \end{array} + \begin{array}{c} \text{within-groups} \\ \text{sum-of-squares} \\ \text{(i.e. error)} \end{array}$$

The between-groups mean-square or estimated variance is its sum-of-squares divided by its degrees of freedom. These degrees of freedom are the number of groups minus one. The degrees of freedom for the total sum-of-squares are the sum of those for the within- and between-groups sum-of-squares or the total number of participants minus one. Although this test may sound complicated, the essential reasoning behind it is that if the groups or samples come from the same population, then the between-groups estimate of the population's variance should be similar to the within-groups estimated variance.

To compare the mean job satisfaction of the four ethnic groups in the Job Survey, we first have to define the groups we want to analyse. As there are no participants identified as 'Other', we have only four groups. If we had a fifth group which we wanted to exclude, we would have to define that group as missing. We then carry out the following procedure:

→**Analyze** →**Compare Means** →**One-Way ANOVA...** [opens **One-Way ANOVA** dialog box shown in Box 7.16]
→**satis** →▸button [puts **satis** under **Dependent List:**] →**ethnicgp** [puts **ethnicgp** under **Factor:**]
→**OK**

The output for this procedure is displayed in Table 7.21. The *F* ratio, which is the between-groups mean-square divided by the within-groups one (2.912/11.289 =0.258), is non-significant. Consequently, there is no significant difference in job satisfaction between the four ethnic groups.

Box 7.16 **One-Way ANOVA** dialog box

Table 7.21 A one-way analysis of variance table comparing job satisfaction across ethnic groups (Job Survey)

ANOVA

SATIS

	Sum of Squares	df	Mean Square	F	Sig.
Between Groups	8.737	3	2.912	.258	.855
Within Groups	722.484	64	11.289		
Total	731.221	67			

The number of cases in each group, their means, standard deviations and the other statistics shown in Table 7.22 are produced by selecting **Options...** (which opens the **One-Way ANOVA: Options** subdialog box shown in Box 7.17) and **Descriptive**.

If we select **Homogeneity-of-variance** in the **Options** subdialog box, Levene's test for homogeneity of variance is produced as shown in Table 7.23. The variances for the four groups do not differ significantly as the significance level is greater than 0.05. If the number of participants in each group and the variances were unequal, it would be necessary to transform the scores so that the variances were equal (see Chapter 9). If it were not possible to make the variances equal, a non-parametric test such as the median or Kruskal–Wallis H test should be used instead.

Table 7.22 Descriptive group statistics with one-way analysis of variance comparing job satisfaction across ethnic groups (Job Survey)

Descriptives

SATIS

	N	Mean	Std. Deviation	Std. Error	95% Confidence Interval for Mean Lower Bound	Upper Bound	Minimum	Maximum
White	35	10.5429	3.2840	.5551	9.4148	11.6710	5.00	19.00
Asian	17	10.9412	3.5964	.8722	9.0921	12.7903	6.00	16.00
West Indian	14	11.2857	3.2917	.8797	9.3852	13.1863	6.00	15.00
African	2	12.0000	2.8284	2.0000	-13.4124	37.4124	10.00	14.00
Total	68	10.8382	3.3036	.4006	10.0386	11.6379	5.00	19.00

Box 7.17 **One-Way ANOVA: Options** subdialog box

Table 7.23 Levene's test of homogeneity of variance (Job Survey)

Test of Homogeneity of Variances

SATIS

Levene Statistic	df1	df2	Sig.
.432	3	64	.731

The *F* test or ratio only tells us whether there is a significant difference between one or more of the groups. It does not inform us where this difference lies. To determine this, we need to carry out further statistical tests. Which tests we use depends on whether or not we have predicted where the differences would be. If, for example, we *predict* that whites would be less satisfied than Asians, then we would carry out an unrelated *t* test as described above using a one-tailed level of significance. We could also do this by selecting the **Contrasts** option which opens the **One-Way ANOVA: Contrasts** subdialog box displayed in Box 7.18. In this option, for instance, we can specify any two groups by defining one of them (that is, whites) as minus one (**–1**), the other one (that is, Asians) as one (**1**), and the remaining ones (that is, West Indians and African) as zeros. To do this, we type **–1** in the box beside **Coefficients:**, select **Add**, type **1** in the box beside **Coefficients:**, select **Add**, type **0** in the box beside **Coefficients:**, select **Add**, type **0** in the box beside **Coefficients:**, select **Add**, type **0** and then **Continue**.

The output for this option is shown in Table 7.24. This gives the value for the contrast, its standard error, and both the pooled and separate variance estimates.

Box 7.18 **One-Way ANOVA: Contrasts** subdialog box

Table 7.24 Statistics provided by a one-way contrast comparing job satisfaction in groups 1 and 2 (Job Survey)

Contrast Coefficients

| Contrast | ETHNICGP | | | |
	White	Asian	West Indian	African
1	-1	1	0	0

Contrast Tests

		Contrast	Value of Contrast	Std. Error	t	df	Sig. (2-tailed)
SATIS	Assume equal variances	1	.3983	.9933	.401	64	.690
	Does not assume equal	1	.3983	1.0339	.385	29.322	.703

However, to determine which of these to use, we need to know whether the variances of the two groups differ. To do this, we obtain the standard deviations as reported in Table 7.22, convert them to variances by squaring them, divide the larger variance by the smaller one ($F = 12.934/10.785 = 1.20$) and look up the result in a table of critical values for F. Alternatively we can do this using Levene's test on the **t-test** procedure. Because the value of the F test is non-significant, we use the pooled variance estimate. The difference in job satisfaction between whites and those of Asian ethnic origin is non-significant.

If, however, we had not expected any differences, then we would need to take into account the fact that if we carried out a large number of comparisons some of these would be significant just by chance. Indeed, at the 5 per cent level of significance, 5 per cent, or one in twenty, comparisons could be expected to be significant by definition. A number of tests which take account of this fact have been developed and are available on the **Post Hoc** option which opens the **One-Way ANOVA: Post Hoc Multiple Comparisons** subdialog box presented in Box 7.19. Because these tests are carried out after the data have been initially analysed, they are referred to as *post hoc* or *a posteriori* tests. One of these, the Scheffé test, will be briefly outlined. This test is the most conservative in the sense that it is least likely to find significant differences between groups or, in other words, to make a Type I error. It is also exact for unequal numbers of participants in the groups. To conduct a Scheffé test to compare job satisfaction between every possible pair of ethnic group, we select **Scheffe** and then **Continue.**

The output for this test is shown in Table 7.25. This shows that there were no significant differences between any of the groups, taken two at a time.

Box 7.19 **One-Way ANOVA: Post Hoc Multiple Comparisons** subdialog box

Table 7.25 Statistics provided by a one-way Scheffé test comparing job satisfaction across ethnic groups (Job Survey)

Multiple Comparisons

Dependent Variable: SATIS
Scheffe

(I) ETHNICGP	(J) ETHNICGP	Mean Difference (I-J)	Std. Error	Sig.	95% Confidence Interval	
					Lower Bound	Upper Bound
White	Asian	-.3983	.9933	.983	-3.2503	2.4537
	West Indian	-.7429	1.0625	.921	-3.7936	2.3079
	African	-1.4571	2.4427	.949	-8.4711	5.5568
Asian	White	.3983	.9933	.983	-2.4537	3.2503
	West Indian	-.3445	1.2126	.994	-3.8263	3.1372
	African	-1.0588	2.5117	.981	-8.2707	6.1530
West Indian	White	.7429	1.0625	.921	-2.3079	3.7936
	Asian	.3445	1.2126	.994	-3.1372	3.8263
	African	-.7143	2.5398	.994	-8.0070	6.5784
African	White	1.4571	2.4427	.949	-5.5568	8.4711
	Asian	1.0588	2.5117	.981	-6.1530	8.2707
	West Indian	.7143	2.5398	.994	-6.5784	8.0070

Homogeneous Subsets

SATIS

Scheffe[a,b]

ETHNICGP	N	Subset for alpha = .05
		1
White	35	10.5429
Asian	17	10.9412
West Indian	14	11.2857
African	2	12.0000
Sig.		.903

Means for groups in homogeneous subsets are displayed.

a. Uses Harmonic Mean Sample Size = 6.071.

b. The group sizes are unequal. The harmonic mean of the group sizes is used. Type 1 error levels are not guaranteed.

Levene's test for three or more unrelated variances

As we have seen, Levene's test is used to determine whether the variances, rather than the means, of three or more unrelated samples are different.

t test for two related means

To compare the means of the same participants in two conditions or at two points in time, we would use a related *t* test. We would also use this test to compare participants who had been matched to be similar in certain respects. The advantage of using the same participants or matched participants is that the amount of error deriving from differences between participants is reduced. The unrelated *t* test compares the mean difference between pairs of scores within the sample with that of the population in terms of the standard error of the difference in means:

$$t = \frac{\text{sample mean differences} - \text{population mean differences}}{\text{standard error of the difference in means}}$$

Since the population mean difference is zero, the closer the sample mean difference is to zero, the less likely it is that the two sets of scores differ significantly from one another.

The difference between a related and an unrelated *t* test lies essentially in the fact that two scores from the same person are likely to vary less than two scores from two different people. For example, if we weigh the same person on two occasions, the difference between those two weights is likely to be less than that between the weights of two separate individuals. This fact is reflected in the different way in which the standard error of the difference in means is calculated for the two tests, which we do not have space to go into here. The variability of the standard error for the related *t* test is less than that for the unrelated one, as illustrated in Figure 7.1. In fact, the variability of the standard error of the difference in means for the related *t* test will depend on the extent to which the pairs of scores are similar or related. The more similar they are, the less the variability of their estimated standard error will be.

To compare two related sets of scores such as job satisfaction in the first two months (**satis1** and **satis2**) in the Panel Study, we would use the following procedure:

→**Analyze** →**Compare Means** →**Paired-Samples T Test…** [opens **Paired-Samples T Test** dialog box shown in Box 7.20]
→**satis1** [puts **satis1** beside **Variable 1:** in **Current Selections** section]
→**satis2** [puts **satis2** beside **Variable 2:** in **Current Selections** section] →
▶button [puts **satis1** and **satis2** under **Paired Variables:**] →**OK**

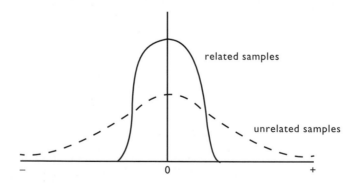

Figure 7.1 A comparison of the distribution of the standard error of the differences in means for related and unrelated samples

Box 7.20 **Paired-Samples T Test** dialog box

This procedure produces the output in Table 7.26. The mean, standard deviation and standard error are given for the two sets of scores as well as for the difference between them. In addition, the extent to which pairs of scores are similar or correlated (see Chapter 8 for an exposition of correlation) is also shown. As can be seen, the correlation between the two sets of scores is significant ($p = 0.029$) but the difference between their means is not significant ($p = 0.742$). In other words, mean job satisfaction does not differ between the first and second month.

Table 7.26 Related *t* test comparing job satisfaction across first two months (Panel Study)

Paired Samples Statistics

		Mean	N	Std. Deviation	Std. Error Mean
Pair 1	SATIS1	11.50	12	3.42	.99
	SATIS2	11.17	12	4.28	1.24

Paired Samples Correlations

		N	Correlation	Sig.
Pair 1	SATIS1 & SATIS2	12	.626	.029

Paired Samples Test

		Paired Differences							
					95% Confidence Interval of the Difference				
		Mean	Std. Deviation	Std. Error Mean	Lower	Upper	t	df	Sig. (2-tailed)
Pair 1	SATIS1 - SATIS2	.33	3.42	.99	-1.84	2.51	.338	11	.742

t test for two related variances

If we want to determine whether the variances of two related samples are significantly different from one another, we have to calculate *t* using the following formula (McNemar, 1969) since it is not available on SPSS:

$$t = \frac{(\text{larger variance} - \text{smaller variance}) \times \sqrt{(\text{number of cases} - 2)}}{\sqrt{\begin{array}{l}(1 - \text{correlation of 2 sets of scores squared}) \\ \quad \times (4 \times \text{larger variance} \times \text{smaller variance})\end{array}}}$$

To apply this formula to the job satisfaction variances in the above example, we would first have to calculate their variances which is the square of their standard deviations (that is, 18.34 and 11.73). Substituting the appropriate values in the above equation, we arrive at a *t* value of 0.91, which with ten degrees of freedom is not significant with a two-tailed test. To have been significant at this level, we would have needed a *t* value of 2.228 or greater.

MULTIVARIATE ANALYSIS OF VARIANCE FOR THREE OR MORE RELATED MEANS

The following section deals with a cluster of procedures that are highly complex and which relate to an application that many readers are unlikely to encounter in the normal course of events. Consequently, this section may be either omitted or returned to after reading Chapter 9.

To compare three or more means from the same or matched participants, such as job satisfaction during three consecutive months, we would need to carry out a multivariate analysis of variance (MANOVA) test which has one within-subjects or *repeated-measures* variable. This variable, job satisfaction, is called a *factor* and has three *levels* since it is repeated three times. This design is referred to variously as a single group (or factor) repeated-measures and treatments-by-subjects design. To conduct it on the present example, we would use the following procedure:

→**Analyze** →**General Linear Model** → **Repeated Measures...** [opens **Repeated Measures Define Factor[s]** dialog box shown in Box 7.21]
→highlight **factor1** type **month** in box beside **Within-Subject Factor Name:**
→box beside **Number of Levels:** and type **3** →**Add** →**Define** [opens **Repeated Measures** subdialog box shown in Box 7.22]
→**satis1** →▶button [puts **satis1** under **Within-Subjects Variables [month]:**]
→**satis2** →▶button →**satis3** →▶button
→**Options** [opens **Repeated Measures: Options** subdialog box shown in Box 7.23] →**Descriptive statistics** →**Continue** [closes **Repeated Measures: Options** subdialog box]
→**OK**

Box 7.21 **Repeated Measures Define Factor[s]** dialog box

Box 7.22 **Repeated Measures** subdialog box

The means and standard deviations of job satisfaction at the three times are shown in Table 7.27. The multivariate tests are presented in Table 7.28. Four multivariate tests are provided to assess the significance of the repeated-measures effect. These are Pillai's criterion, Hotelling's trace criterion, Wilks' Lambda, and Roy's *gcr* criterion. In many cases, all four tests give the same results (Stevens, 1996). Provided that the number of participants in each group is equal or almost equal, it does not matter which test is used. Where this is not the case, Pillai's criterion may be the most appropriate.

Repeated Measures: Options

Estimated Marginal Means

Factor(s) and Factor Interactions:

(OVERALL)
month

Display Means for:

☐ Compare main effects

Confidence interval adjustment:

LSD (none)

Display

☑ Descriptive statistics
☐ Estimates of effect size
☐ Observed power
☐ Parameter estimates
☐ SSCP matrices
☐ Residual SSCP matrix

☐ Transformation matrix
☐ Homogeneity tests
☐ Spread vs. level plots
☐ Residual plots
☐ Lack of fit test
☐ General estimable function

Significance level: .05   Confidence intervals are 95%

Continue   Cancel   Help

Box 7.23 **Repeated Measures: Options** subdialog box

Table 7.27 Repeated measures means and standard deviations
for job satisfaction (Panel Study)

Descriptive Statistics

	Mean	Std. Deviation	N
SATIS1	11.50	3.42	12
SATIS2	11.17	4.28	12
SATIS3	10.75	3.22	12

Table 7.28 Repeated measures multivariate tests (Panel Study)

Multivariate Tests[b]

Effect		Value	F	Hypothesis df	Error df	Sig.
MONTH	Pillai's Trace	.075	.404[a]	2.000	10.000	.678
	Wilks' Lambda	.925	.404[a]	2.000	10.000	.678
	Hotelling's Trace	.081	.404[a]	2.000	10.000	.678
	Roy's Largest Root	.081	.404[a]	2.000	10.000	.678

a. Exact statistic
b.
   Design: Intercept
   Within Subjects Design: MONTH

The output for Mauchly's test of sphericity is presented in Table 7.29. Because this test is not significant we assume sphericity and look at the output in the first line of the table in Table 7.31. If the test had been significant, the significance of the F ratio needs to be adjusted with one of the three adjustments offered.

The univariate tests are for the two transformed variables, T2 and T3, shown in Table 7.30. It is important to note that T2 and T3 do not refer to the original variables with those names, but to the two transformed variables. When comparing three related scores, it is only necessary to test the statistical significance of the differences between two of them (for example, **satis1** – **satis2** and **satis2** – **satis3**) since the remaining difference (that is, **satis1** – **satis3**) can be worked out if the other two differences are known [(**satis1** – **satis3**) = (**satis1** – **satis2**) + (**satis2** – **satis3**)]. The number of unrelated comparisons is always one less than the number of variables being compared. Unless requested otherwise, SPSS automatically transforms the variables in a repeated-measures design so that the comparisons are statistically independent. The nature of these transformations can be determined by examining the transformation matrix. However, this is normally done only when the univariate tests are significant, which is not the case here. The values for both the multivariate and univariate tests are not significant. In other words, there is no difference in mean job satisfaction over the three months.

Table 7.29 Repeated measures Mauchly's test of sphericity (Panel Study)

Mauchly's Test of Sphericity[b]

Measure: MEASURE_1

Within Subjects Effect	Mauchly's W	Approx Chi-Square	df	Sig.	Epsilon[a]		
					Greenhouse-Geisser	Huynh-Feldt	Lower-bound
MONTH	.882	1.253	2	.533	.895	1.000	.500

Tests the null hypothesis that the error covariance matrix of the orthonormalized transformed dependent variables is proportional to an identity matrix.

a. May be used to adjust the degrees of freedom for the averaged tests of significance. Corrected tests are displayed in the Tests of Within-Subjects Effects table.

b.
   Design: Intercept
   Within Subjects Design: MONTH

Table 7.30 Repeated measures univariate tests of significance for transformed variables (Panel Study)

Tests of Within-Subjects Contrasts

Measure: Measure_1

Source	MONTH	Type III Sum of Squares	df	Mean Square	F	Sig.
MONTH	Linear	3.375	1	3.375	.881	.368
	Quadratic	1.389E-02	1	1.389E-02	.002	.966
Error(MONTH)	Linear	42.125	11	3.830		
	Quadratic	81.153	11	7.378		

Table 8.5 Contingency table: **skill** by **gender** (SPSS output)

SKILL * GENDER Crosstabulation

			GENDER		
			men	women	Total
SKILL	unskilled	Count	5	9	14
		% within SKILL	35.7%	64.3%	100.0%
		% within GENDER	12.8%	29.0%	20.0%
	semi-skilled	Count	11	7	18
		% within SKILL	61.1%	38.9%	100.0%
		% within GENDER	28.2%	22.6%	25.7%
	fairly skilled	Count	11	10	21
		% within SKILL	52.4%	47.6%	100.0%
		% within GENDER	28.2%	32.3%	30.0%
	highly skilled	Count	12	5	17
		% within SKILL	70.6%	29.4%	100.0%
		% within GENDER	30.8%	16.1%	24.3%
Total		Count	39	31	70
		% within SKILL	55.7%	44.3%	100.0%
		% within GENDER	100.0%	100.0%	100.0%

Chi-Square Tests

	Value	df	Asymp. Sig. (2-sided)
Pearson Chi-Square	4.101[a]	3	.251
Likelihood Ratio	4.157	3	.245
Linear-by-Linear Association	2.591	1	.107
N of Valid Cases	70		

a. 0 cells (.0%) have expected count less than 5. The minimum expected count is 6.20.

Symmetric Measures

		Value	Approx. Sig.
Nominal by Nominal	Phi	.242	.251
	Cramer's V	.242	.251
N of Valid Cases		70	

a. Not assuming the null hypothesis.
b. Using the asymptotic standard error assuming the null hypothesis.

only afflicts those who smoke. If there had been a perfect relationship between satisfaction and absence, the contingency table presented in Table 8.4a would be in evidence; if there was no relationship, the crosstabulation in Table 8.4b would be expected. In the case of Table 8.4a, all individuals who express satisfaction would be in the 'No' category, and all who are not satisfied would be in the absence category. With Table 8.4b, those who are not satisfied are equally likely to have been absent as not absent.

As noted above, the percentages in Tables 8.2 to 8.4 are column percentages. Another kind of percentage that might have been preferred is a row percentage. With this calculation, the frequency in each cell is calculated in terms of the row totals, so that the percentage for cell 1 would be $4/15 \times 100$, that is, 27 per cent. The row percentages for cells 2, 3 and 4 respectively would be 73 per cent, 67 per cent and 33 per cent. In taking row percentages, we would be emphasising a different aspect of the table, for example, the percentage of those who have been absent who are satisfied (27 per cent in cell 1) and the percentage who are not satisfied with their jobs (73 per cent in cell 2). The question of whether to use row or column percentages in part depends on what aspects of the data you want to highlight. It is sometimes suggested that the decision depends on whether the independent variable is across the top or along the side of the table: if the former, column percentages should be used; if the latter, row percentages should be employed. Typically, the independent variable will go across the table, in which case column percentages should be used. However, this suggestion implies that there is a straightforward means of identifying the independent and dependent variables, but this is not always the case and great caution should be exercised in making such an inference, for reasons that will be explored below. It may appear that job satisfaction is the independent and absence the dependent variable, but it is hazardous to make such an attribution.

SPSS can produce tables without percentages, though such tables are unlikely to be very helpful, and can produce output with either row or column percentages or both.

Crosstabulation with SPSS

Crosstabulations can easily be created with SPSS. Let us turn now to the Job Survey data. Imagine that we want to examine the relationship between **skill** and **gender** and that we want the following information in the table: counts (that is, the frequency for each cell); the row percentages; the column percentages; and a chi-square test. This last piece of information will be dealt with in detail below. Let us also say that we want the dependent variable, **skill**, to go down the table and the independent variable, **gender**, to go across. To produce such output (see Table 8.5), the following sequence should be followed:

→**Analyze** →**Descriptive Statistics** →**Crosstabs...** [opens **Crosstabs** dialog box shown in Box 8.1]
→**skill** →▶button [puts **income** in **Row[s]:** box] →**gender** →▶button [puts **gender** in **Column[s]:** box] →**Statistics...** [opens **Crosstabs: Statistics** subdialog box shown in Box 8.2]
→**Chi-square** →**Continue** [closes **Crosstabs: Statistics** dialog box]
→**Cells...** [opens **Crosstabs: Cell Display** subdialog box shown in Box 8.3] [ensure **Observed** beneath **Counts** has been selected. Under **Percentages** ensure **Row** and **Column** have been selected.] →**Continue**
→**OK**

Table 8.8 Matrix of Spearman's rho correlation coefficients

Correlations

			SKILL	PRODY	QUAL
Spearman's rho	SKILL	Correlation Coefficient	1.000	.239*	.013
		Sig. (2-tailed)	.	.048	.913
		N	70	69	70
	PRODY	Correlation Coefficient	.239*	1.000	.171
		Sig. (2-tailed)	.048	.	.160
		N	69	69	69
	QUAL	Correlation Coefficient	.013	.171	1.000
		Sig. (2-tailed)	.913	.160	.
		N	70	69	70

*. Correlation is significant at the .05 level (2-tailed).

researchers, it is probably preferable to report this statistic unless there are obvious reasons for thinking otherwise. One possible reason that is sometimes suggested for preferring tau is that it deals better with tied ranks – for example, where two or more people are at the same rank. Thus, if there seem to be quite a large proportion of tied ranks, tau may be preferable.

Let us say that we want to correlate **skill**, **prody** and **qual**, each of which is an ordinal measure. Even though these are ordinal variables, they have to be rank ordered. SPSS allows both tau and rho to be computed. The procedure is essentially identical to that used above for generating Pearson's r, except that it is necessary to select Kendall's tau or Spearman's rho or both. Thus the sequence is:

→**Analyze** →**Correlate** →**Bivariate...** [opens **Bivariate Correlations** dialog box shown in Box 8.6]
→**qual** →▶button →**prody** →▶button →**skill** →▶button [puts **qual**, **prody** and **skill** into **Variables** box] →**Kendall's tau-b** [*if* not already selected] or **Spearman** or both →**One-tailed** [*if* preferred to **Two-tailed**] →**OK**

It will also be necessary to decide whether to exclude missing cases on a listwise or pairwise basis through the **Options** button. Table 8.8 shows the output for Spearman's rho only. All of the correlations reported in Table 8.8 are low, the largest being the correlation between **prody** and **skill** (0.24 rounded up). This is the only one of the three correlations that achieves statistical significance at $p < 0.05$. Thus, there is a tendency for better skilled workers to be more productive.

Although rank correlation methods are more flexible than Pearson's r, the latter tends to be preferred because interval/ratio variables comprise more information than ordinal ones. One of the reasons for the widespread use in the social sciences of questionnaire items which are built up into scales or indices (and which are then treated as interval variables) is probably that stronger approaches to the investigation of relationships like Pearson's r (and regression – see below) can be employed.

OTHER APPROACHES TO BIVARIATE RELATIONSHIPS

Up to now, the approach to the examination of relationships has been undertaken within a framework in which the nature of the variables has been the most important factor: crosstabulation and chi-square are most likely to occur in conjunction with nominal variables; Pearson's r presumes the use of interval variables; and when examining pairs of ordinal variables, rho or tau should be employed. However, what if, as can easily occur in the social sciences, pairs of variables are of different types, for example nominal plus ordinal or ordinal plus interval? There are methods for the elucidation of relationships which can deal with such eventualities. Freeman (1965), for example, catalogues a vast array of methods that can be used in such circumstances. There are problems with many of these methods. First, they are unfamiliar to most readers, who would therefore experience great difficulty in understanding and interpreting the results of calculations. Second, while particular statistical methods should not be followed fetishistically, the notion of learning a new statistical method each time a particular combination of circumstances arises is also not ideal. Third, for many unusual methods software is not available, even within a wide-ranging package like SPSS.

One rule of thumb that can be recommended is to move downwards in measurement level when confronted with a pair of different variables. Thus, if you have an ordinal and an interval variable, a method of rank correlation could be used. If you have an ordinal and a nominal variable, you should use crosstabulation and chi-square. This may mean collapsing ranks into groups (for example, 1–5, 6–10, 11–15, and so on) and assigning ranks to the groupings (for example, 1–5 = 1, 6–10 = 2, 11–15 = 3, and so on), using the **Recode** procedure. If you have a nominal and an interval variable, again the combination of a contingency table and chi-square is likely to be used. As suggested in the discussion of crosstabulation, the interval variable will need to be collapsed into groups. The chief source of concern with collapsing values of an ordinal or interval variable is that the choice of cut-off points is bound to be arbitrary and will have a direct impact on the results obtained. Accordingly, it may be better to use more than one method of grouping or to employ a fairly systematic procedure such as quartiles as a means of collapsing cases into four groups.

When pairs of variables are dichotomous, the phi coefficient should be given serious consideration. Its interpretation is the same as Pearson's r, in that it varies between 0 and +1. A description of a test of statistical significance for phi was provided in the section on crosstabulation. Phi represents something of a puzzle. Some text-books indicate that phi can take a positive or negative value, which means that it can measure both the strength and the direction of relationships among dichotomous variables. However, the phi coefficient that is generated by SPSS can only assume a positive value. The reason for this apparent inconsistency lies in the different formulae that are employed.

Statistics textbooks often present a host of methods for examining relationships

Table 8.9 **Means** output for **satis** by **skill**

Report

SATIS

SKILL	Mean	N	Std. Deviation
unskilled	8.64	14	2.50
semi-skilled	9.67	18	2.40
fairly skilled	11.79	19	3.38
highly skilled	12.82	17	3.26
Total	10.84	68	3.30

ANOVA Table

			Sum of Squares	df	Mean Square	F	Sig.
job satisfaction * SKILL	Between Groups	(Combined)	176.378	3	58.793	6.782	.000
	Within Groups		554.843	64	8.669		
	Total		731.221	67			

Measures of Association

	Eta	Eta Squared
SATIS * SKILL	.491	.241

[ensure **Mean, Standard Deviation** and **Number of Cases** appear in the <u>C</u>ell
Statistics: box] →<u>A</u>**nova table and eta** in the **Statistics for First Layer** box
→**Continue** [closes **Means: Options** subdialog box]
→**OK**

An analysis of variance table will be produced along with the *F* ratio (which
provides a test of statistical significance), and eta and eta-squared. Table 8.9
provides SPSS output from this set of commands. As this output shows, job satisfaction varies by skill (with lower **satis** means for lower **skill** levels) and the *F*
ratio of 6.782 is significant at the 0.0005 level, suggesting a strong probability of a
relationship in the population. The eta-squared suggests that about one-quarter
of the variance of **satis** can be attributed to **skill.** Thus, **Means...** can be considered
a useful tool for examining relationships when there is an interval dependent
variable and a nominal, dichotomous, or short ordinal variable. However, it only
makes sense if the interval variable can be unambiguously recognised as the
dependent variable.

REGRESSION

Regression has become one of the most widely used techniques in the analysis of
data in the social sciences. It is closely connected to Pearson's *r*, as will become
apparent at a number of points. Indeed, it shares many of the same assumptions as

r, such as that relationships between variables are linear and that variables are interval. In this section, the use of regression to explore relationships between pairs of variables will be examined. It should become apparent that regression is a powerful tool for summarising the nature of the relationship between variables and for making predictions of likely values of the dependent variable.

At this point, it is worth returning to the scatter diagrams encountered in Figures 8.1 and 8.2. Each departs a good deal from Figure 8.3 in which all of the points are on a straight line, since the points in Figures 8.1 and 8.2 are more scattered. The idea of regression is to summarise the relationship between two variables by producing a line which fits the data closely. This line is called the *line of best fit*. Only one line will minimise the deviations of all of the dots in a scatter diagram from the line. Some points will appear above the line, some below and a small proportion may actually be on the line. Because only one line can meet the criterion of line of best fit, it is unlikely that it can be drawn accurately by visual inspection. This is where regression comes in. Regression procedures allow the precise line of best fit to be computed. Once we know the line of best fit, we can make predictions about likely values of the dependent variable, for particular values of the independent variable.

In order to understand how the line of best fit operates, it is necessary to get to grips with the simple equation that governs its operation and how we make predictions from it. The equation is:

$$y = a + bx + e$$

In this equation, y and x are the dependent and independent variables respectively. The two elements – a and b – refer to aspects of the line itself. First, a is known as the intercept, which is the point at which the line cuts the vertical axis. Second, b is the slope of the line of best fit and is usually referred to as the regression coefficient. By the 'slope' is meant the rate at which changes in values of the independent variable (x) affect values of the dependent variable (y). In order to predict y for a given value of x, it is necessary to:

1 multiply the value of x by the regression coefficient, b; and
2 add this calculation to the intercept, a.

Finally, e is referred to as an *error term*, which points to the fact that a proportion of the variance in the dependent variable, y, is unexplained by the regression equation. In order to simplify the following explanation of regression, for the purposes of making predictions the error term is ignored and so will not be referred to below.

Consider the following example. A researcher may want to know whether managers who put in extra hours after the normal working day tend to get on better in the organisation than others. The researcher finds out the average amount of time a group of twenty new managers in a firm spend working on problems after normal working hours. Two years later the managers are re-examined to find out their annual salaries. Individuals' salaries are employed as an indicator of progress, since incomes often reflect how well a person is getting on in a firm.

Figure 8.10 A line of best fit

Moreover, for these managers, extra hours of work are not rewarded by overtime payments, so salaries are a real indication of progress. Let us say that the regression equation which is derived from the analysis is:

$$y = 7500 + 500x$$

The line of best fit is drawn in Figure 8.10.

The intercept, a, is 7500, that is, £7500; the regression coefficient, b, is 500, that is, £500. The latter means that each extra hour worked produces an extra £500 on a manager's annual salary. We can calculate the likely annual salary of someone who puts in an extra 7 hours per week as follows:

$$y = 7500 + (500)(7)$$

which becomes:

$$y = 7500 + 3500$$

which becomes:

$$y = 11000 \text{ (that is, £11,000).}$$

For someone who works an extra 8 hours per week, the likely salary will be £11,500, that is, 7500 + (500)(8). If a person does not put in any extra work, the

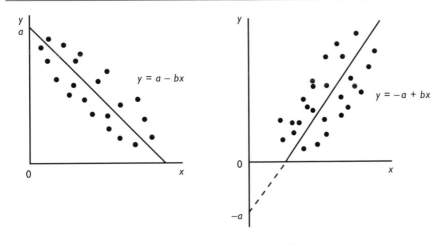

Figure 8.11 Regression: a negative relationship

Figure 8.12 Regression: a negative intercept

salary is likely to be £7,500, that is, 7500 + (500)(0). Thus, through regression, we are able to show how y changes for each additional increment of x (because the regression coefficient expresses how much more of y you get for each extra increment of x) and to predict the likely value of y for a given value of x. When a relationship is negative, the regression equation for the line of best fit will take the form $y = a - bx$ (see Figure 8.11). Thus, if a regression equation is $y = 50 - 2x$, each extra increment of x produces a decrease in y. If we wanted to know the likely value of y when $x = 12$, we would substitute as follows:

$y = 50 - 2x$
$y = 50 - (2)(12)$
$y = 50 - 24$
$y = 26.$

When a line of best fit shows a tendency to be vertical and to intersect with the horizontal axis, the intercept, a, will have a minus value. This is because it will cut the horizontal axis and when extended to the vertical axis it will intercept it at a negative point (see Figure 8.12). In this situation, the regression equation will take the form:

$y = -a + bx$

Supposing the equation were $y = -7 + 23x$; if we wanted to know the likely value of y when $x = 3$, we would substitute as follows:

$y = -7 + 23x$
$y = -7 + (23)(3)$
$y = -7 + 69$
$y = 69 - 7$
$y = 62.$

Figure 8.13 Regression: a perfect
relationship

Figure 8.14 The accuracy of the line of
best fit

As suggested at the start of this section, correlation and regression are closely connected. They make identical assumptions that variables are interval/ratio and that relationships are linear. Further, r and r^2 are often employed as indications of how well the regression line fits the data. For example, if $r=1$, the line of best fit would simply be drawn straight through all of the points (see Figure 8.13). Where points are more scattered, the line of best fit will provide a poorer fit with the data. Accordingly, the more scatter there is in a scatter diagram, the less accurate the prediction of likely y values will be. Thus, the closer r is to 1, the less scatter there is and, therefore, the better the fit between the line of best fit and the data. If the two scatter diagrams in Figures 8.6 and 8.7 are examined, the line of best fit for the left-hand diagram in each case will constitute a superior fit between data and line and will permit more accurate predictions. This can be further illustrated by reference to Figure 8.14. If we take a particular value of x, that is, x_n, then we can estimate the likely value of y (y_n) from the regression line. However, the corresponding y value for a particular case may be y_n, which is different from y. In other words, the latter provides an estimate of y, which is likely to be not totally accurate. Clearly, the further the points are from the line, the less accurate estimates are likely to be. Therefore, where r is low, scatter will be greater and the regression equation will provide a less accurate representation of the relationship between the two variables.

On the other hand, although correlation and regression are closely connected, it should be remembered that they serve different purposes. Correlation is concerned with the degrees of relationship between variables, and regression with making predictions. But they can also be usefully used in conjunction, since, unlike correlation, regression can express the character of relationships. Compare the two scatter diagrams in Figure 8.15. The pattern of dots is identical and each would reveal an identical level of correlation (say 0.75), but the slope of the dots in (a) is much steeper than in (b). This difference would be revealed in a larger regression coefficient for (a) and a larger intercept for (b).

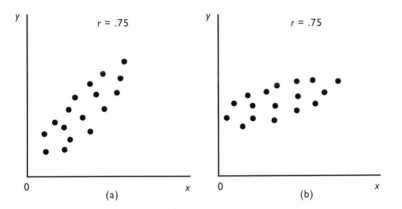

Figure 8.15 Scatter diagrams for two identical levels of correlation

The r^2 value is often used as an indication of how well the model implied by the regression equation fits the data. If we conceive of y, the dependent variable, as exhibiting variance which the independent variable goes some of the way in explaining, then we can say that r^2 reflects the proportion of the variation in y explained by x. Thus, if r^2 equals 0.74, the model is providing an explanation of 74 per cent of the variance in y.

Although we have been talking about y as the dependent and x as the independent variable, in many instances it makes just as much sense to treat x as dependent and y as independent. If this is done, the regression equation will be different. Two other words of caution should be registered. First, regression assumes that the dispersion of points in a scatter diagram is *homoscedastic*, or where the pattern of scatter of the points about the line shows no clear pattern. When the opposite is the case, and the pattern exhibits *heteroscedasticity*, where the amount of scatter around the line of best fit varies markedly at different points, the use of regression

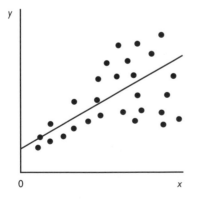

Figure 8.16 Heteroscedasticity

is questionable. An example of heteroscedasticity is exhibited in Figure 8.16, which suggests that the amount of unexplained variation exhibited by the model is greater at the upper reaches of *x* and *y*. Homoscedasticity is also a precondition of the use of Pearson's *r*.

Second, the size of a correlation coefficient and the nature of a regression equation will be affected by the amount of variance in either of the variables concerned. For example, if one variable has a restricted range and the other a wider range, the size of the correlation coefficient may be reduced, compared with if both were of equally wide variance.

Third, *outliers*, that is extreme values of *x* or *y*, can exert an excessive influence on the results of both correlation and regression. Consider the data in Table 8.10. We have data on twenty firms regarding their size (as measured by the number of employees) and the number of specialist functions in the organisation (that is, the number of specialist areas, such as accounting, personnel, marketing or public relations, in which at least one person spends 100 per cent of his or her time). The article by Child (1973) presents a similar variable with a maximum score of 16,

Table 8.10 The impact of an outlier: the relationship between size of firm and number of specialist functions

Case number	Size of firm (number of employees)	Number of specialist functions
1	110	3
2	150	2
3	190	5
4	230	8
5	270	5
6	280	6
7	320	7
8	350	5
9	370	8
10	390	6
11	420	9
12	430	7
13	460	3
14	470	9
15	500	12
16	540	9
17	550	13
18	600	14
19	640	11
20	2,700	16

Notes:
When case 20 is included, Pearson's *r* = 0.67 and the regression equation is: specialisation = 5.55 + 0.00472size.
When case 20 is excluded, Pearson's *r* = 0.78 and the regression equation is: specialisation = 0.78 + 0.0175size.

which formed the idea for this example. In Table 8.10, we have an outlier – case number 20 – which is much larger than all the other firms in the sample. It is also somewhat higher in terms of the number of specialist functions than the other firms. In spite of the fact that this is only one case, its impact on estimates of both correlation and regression is quite pronounced. The Pearson's r is 0.67 and the regression equation is $y = 5.55 + 0.00472size$. If the case with the outlier is excluded, the magnitude of r rises to 0.78 and the regression equation is $y = 0.78 + 0.0175size$. Such a difference can have a dramatic effect on predictions. If we wanted to know the likely value of y (number of specialist functions) for an organisation of 340 employees with all twenty cases, the prediction would be 7.15; with the outlying case omitted the prediction is 6.73. Thus, this one outlying case can have an important impact upon the predictions that are generated. When such a situation arises, serious consideration has to be given to the exclusion of such an outlying case.

The purpose of this section has been to introduce the general idea of regression. In Chapter 10, it will receive much fuller treatment, when the use of more than one independent variable will be examined, an area in which the power of regression is especially evident.

Generating basic regression analysis with SPSS

SPSS can generate a host of information relating to regression. However, much of this information is too detailed for present purposes; only some of it will be examined in Chapter 10. It is proposed to postpone a detailed treatment of generating regression information until this later chapter. The following discussion should allow the user to generate basic regression information relating to the relationship between two variables. Imagine that we want to undertake a simple regression analysis of **routine** and **satis**, with the latter as the implied dependent variable. The following sequence should be followed:

→**Statistics** →**Regression** →**Linear...** [opens **Linear Regression** dialog box shown in Box 8.9]
→**satis** →▶button [puts **satis** in **Dependent:** box] →**routine** →▶button [puts **routine** in **Independent[s]:** box] →**OK**

The regression equation can be found below **Variables in the Equation** in the resulting output (see Table 8.11). The equation is:

satis = 17.094 – 0.464**routine**

which can be rounded to:

satis = 17.09 – 0.46**routine**

Box 8.9 **Linear Regression** dialog box

This implies that for every increment of **routine**, **satis** declines by 0.46. We are also given quite a large amount of extra information. We are given the coefficient of determination, r^2, which is 0.336 (see **R Square**), which implies that 33.6 per cent of the variance in **satis** is explained by **routine**. Other basic useful information includes an estimation of the statistical significance of the coefficients relating to the constant in the equation and to **routine** using the t value and an analysis of variance which provides an F test for the equation. The p values suggest that the coefficients and the equation itself achieve a high level of statistical significance.

A scatter diagram along with a fitted regression line and basic regression information can be generated in SPSS. To generate this output, a scatter diagram needs to be produced as above, using the sequence previously followed:

→**Graphs** →**Scatter...** [opens **Scatterplot** dialog box shown in Box 8.4]
→**Simple** →**Define** [closes **Scatterplot** dialog box and opens **Simple Scatterplot** dialog box shown in Box 8.5]
→**satis** →▶button [puts **satis** in box by **Y Axis:**] →**routine** →▶button [puts **routine** in box by **X Axis:**] →**OK**

When the diagram has appeared:

Table 8.11 Regression analysis: **satis** by **routine** (SPSS output)

Variables Entered/Removed[b]

Model	Variables Entered	Variables Removed	Method
1	ROUTINE[a]	.	Enter

a. All requested variables entered.
b. Dependent Variable: SATIS

Model Summary

Model	R	R Square	Adjusted R Square	Std. Error of the Estimate
1	.580[a]	.336	.326	2.71

a. Predictors: (Constant), ROUTINE

ANOVA[b]

Model		Sum of Squares	df	Mean Square	F	Sig.
1	Regression	246.036	1	246.036	33.469	.000[a]
	Residual	485.184	66	7.351		
	Total	731.221	67			

a. Predictors: (Constant), ROUTINE
b. Dependent Variable: SATIS

Coefficients[a]

Model		Unstandardized Coefficients B	Std. Error	Standardized Coefficients Beta	t	Sig.
1	(Constant)	17.094	1.130		15.125	.000
	ROUTINE	-.464	.080	-.580	-5.785	.000

a. Dependent Variable: SATIS

double-click anywhere in the scatterplot [opens **SPSS Chart Editor** and the main figure becomes shaded] →**C**hart →**O**ptions... [opens **Scatterplot Options** subdialog box]
→**T**otal under **Fit Line** →**OK**

A regression line will be drawn on to the scatter diagram. Figure 8.17 provides an example of a scatter diagram with a line of best fit produced with SPSS.

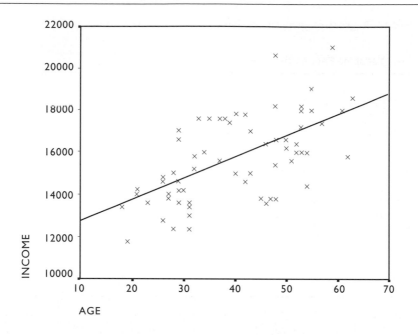

Figure 8.17 SPSS scatter diagram with line of best fit (Job Survey data)

OVERVIEW OF TYPES OF VARIABLE AND METHODS OF EXAMINING RELATIONSHIPS

The following rules of thumb are suggested for the various types of combination of variable that may occur:

1   Nominal–nominal. Contingency-table analysis in conjunction with chi-square as a test of statistical significance can be recommended. To test for strength of association, Cramer's *V* can be used.
2   Ordinal–ordinal. Spearman's rho or Kendall's tau and their associated significance tests.
3   Interval–interval. Pearson's *r* and regression for estimates of the strength and character of relationships respectively. Each can generate tests of statistical significance, but more detail in this regard for regression is provided in Chapter 10.
4   Dichotomous–dichotomous. Same as under 1 for nominal–nominal, except that phi should be used instead of Cramer's *V* (and will be generated by SPSS instead of *V*).
5   Interval–ordinal. If the ordinal variable assumes quite a large number of categories, it will probably be best to use rho or tau. Contingency-table analysis may be used if there are few categories in both the ordinal and interval variables (or if categories can meaningfully be 'grouped'). If the interval vari-

able can be relatively unambiguously identified as the dependent variable and if the ordinal variable has few categories, another approach may be to use the **Means...** procedure and to request an analysis of variance which will in turn allow an F ratio to be computed. In this way, a test of statistical significance can be provided, along with eta-squared.

6   Interval–nominal or interval–dichotomous. Contingency-table analysis plus the use of chi-square may be employed if the interval variable can be sensibly 'collapsed' into categories. This approach is appropriate if it is not meaning-ful to talk about which is the independent and which is the dependent variable. If the interval variable can be identified as a dependent variable, the **Means...** procedure and its associated statistics should be considered.

7   Nominal–ordinal. Same as 1.

EXERCISES

1   (a) Using SPSS, how would you create a contingency table for the relation-ship between **gender** and **prody**, with the former variable going across, along with column percentages (Job Survey data)?
    (b) How would you assess the statistical significance of the relationship with SPSS?
    (c) In your view, is the relationship statistically significant?
    (d) What is the percentage of women who are described as exhibiting 'good' productivity?

2   A researcher carries out a study of the relationship between ethnic group and voting behaviour. The relationship is examined through a contingency table, for which the researcher computes the chi-square statistic. The value of chi-square turns out to be statistically significant at $p < 0.01$. The researcher concludes that this means that the relationship between the two variables is important and strong. Assess this reasoning.

3   (a) Using SPSS, how would you generate a matrix of Pearson's r correlation coefficients for **income**, **years**, **satis** and **age** (Job Survey data)?
    (b) Conduct an analysis using the commands from question 3 (a). Which pair of variables exhibits the largest correlation?
    (c) Taking this pair of variables, how much of the variance in one variable is explained by the other?

4   A researcher wants to examine the relationship between social class and number of books read in a year. The first hundred people are interviewed as they enter a public library in the researcher's home town. On the basis of the answers given, the sample is categorised in terms of a four-fold classification of social class: upper middle class/lower middle class/ upper working class/ lower working class. Using Pearson's r, the level of correlation is found to be 0.73 which is significant at $p < 0.001$. The researcher concludes that the find-

ings have considerable validity, especially since 73 per cent of the variance in number of books read is explained by social class. Assess the researcher's analysis and conclusions.

5   A researcher finds that the correlation between income and a scale measuring interest in work is 0.55 (Pearson's r) which is non-significant since p is greater than 0.05. This finding is compared to another study using the same variables and measures which found the correlation to be 0.46 and $p < 0.001$. How could this contrast arise? In other words, how could the larger correlation be non-significant and the smaller correlation be significant?

6   (a) What statistic or statistics would you recommend to estimate the strength of the relationship between **prody** and **commit** (Job Survey data)?
     (b) What SPSS commands would you use to generate the relevant estimates?
     (c) What is the result of using these commands?

7   The regression equation for the relationship between **age** and **autonom** (with the latter as the dependent variable) is **autonom** = 6.964 + 0.06230**age** $r = 0.28$.
     (a) Explain what 6.964 means.
     (b) Explain what 0.06230 means.
     (c) How well does the regression equation fit the data?
     (d) What is the likely level of **autonom** for someone aged 54?
     (e) Using SPSS, how would you generate this regression information?

Chapter 9

Multivariate analysis

Exploring differences among three or more variables

In most studies in the social sciences we collect information on more than just two variables. Although it would be possible and more simple to examine the relationships between these variables just two at a time, there are serious disadvantages to restricting oneself to this approach, as we shall see. It is preferable initially to explore these data with multivariate rather than bivariate tests. The reasons for looking at three or more variables vary according to the aims and design of a study. Consequently, we shall begin by outlining four design features which only involve three variables at a time. Obviously these features may include more than three variables and the features themselves can be combined to form more complicated designs, but we shall discuss them largely as if they were separate designs. However, as has been done before, we shall use one set of data to illustrate their analysis, all of which can be carried out with a general statistical model called *multivariate analysis of variance and covariance* (MANOVA and MANCOVA). This model requires the Advanced Statistics option. Although the details of the model are difficult to understand and to convey simply (and so will not be attempted here), its basic principles are similar to those of other parametric tests we have previously discussed such as the *t* test, one-way analysis of variance and simple regression.

MULTIVARIATE DESIGNS

Factorial design

We are often interested in the effect of two variables on a third, particularly if we believe that the two variables may influence one another. To take a purely hypothetical case, we may expect the gender of the patient to interact with the kind of treatment they are given for feeling depressed. Women may respond more positively to psychotherapy where they have an opportunity to talk about their feelings while men may react more favourably to being treated with an antidepressant drug. In this case, we are anticipating that the kind of treatment will *interact* with gender in alleviating depression. An interaction is when the effect of one variable

Figure 9.1 An example of an interaction between two variables

is not the same under all the conditions of the other variable. It is often more readily understood when it is depicted in the form of a graph as in Figure 9.1. However, whether these effects are statistically significant can only be determined by testing them and not just by visually inspecting them. The vertical axis shows the amount of improvement in depression that has taken place after treatment, while the horizontal one can represent either of the other two variables. In this case it reflects the kind of treatment received. The effect of the third variable, gender, is depicted by two different kinds of points and lines in the graph itself. Men are indicated by a cross and a continuous line while women are signified by a small circle and a broken line.

An interaction is indicated when the two lines representing the third variable are not parallel. Consequently, a variety of interaction effects can exist, three of which are shown in Figure 9.2 as hypothetical possibilities. In Figure 9.2a, men show less improvement with psychotherapy than with drugs while women derive greater benefit from psychotherapy than from the drug treatment. In Figure 9.2b, men improve little with either treatment, while women, once again, benefit considerably more from psychotherapy than from drugs. Finally, in Figure 9.2c, both men and women improve more with psychotherapy than with drugs, but the improvement is much greater for women than it is for men.

The absence of an interaction can be seen by the lines representing the third

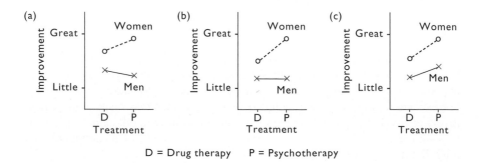

Figure 9.2 Examples of other interactions

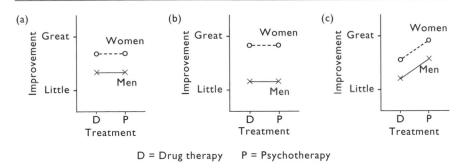

D = Drug therapy   P = Psychotherapy

Figure 9.3 Examples of no interactions

variable remaining more or less parallel to one another, as is the case in the three examples in Figure 9.3. In Figure 9.3a, both men and women show a similar degree of improvement with both treatments. In Figure 9.3b, women improve more than men under both conditions while both treatments are equally effective. In Figure 9.3c, women show greater benefit than men with both treatments, and psychotherapy is better than drugs.

The results of treatment and gender on their own are known as *main* effects. In these situations, the influence of the other variable is disregarded. If, for example, we want to examine the effect of gender, we would only look at improvement for men and women, ignoring treatment. If we are interested in the effect of the kind of treatment, we would simply compare the outcome of patients receiving psychotherapy with those being given drugs, paying no heed to gender.

The variables which are used to form the comparison groups are termed *factors*. The number of groups which constitute a factor are referred to as the *levels* of that factor. Since gender consists of two groups, it is called a two-level factor. The two kinds of treatment also create a two-level factor. If a third treatment had been included such as a control group of patients receiving neither drugs nor psychotherapy, we would have a three-level factor. Studies which investigate the effects of two or more factors are known as *factorial* designs. A study comparing two levels of gender and two levels of treatment is described as a *2×2* factorial design. If three rather than two levels of treatment had been compared, it would be a 2×3 factorial design. A study which only looks at one factor is called a one-way or single factor design.

The factors in these designs may be ones that are *manipulated*, such as differing dosages of drugs, different teaching methods, or varying levels of induced anxiety. Where they have been manipulated and where participants have been randomly assigned to different levels, the factors may also be referred to as *independent* variables since they are more likely to be unrelated to, or independent of, other features of the experimental situation such as the personality of the participants. Variables which are used to assess the effect of these independent variables are known as *dependent* variables since the effect on them is thought to depend on the level of the variable which has been manipulated. Thus, for example, the improvement in the depression experienced by patients (that is, the dependent variable) is believed to be partly the result of the treatment they have received (that is, the independent variable). Factors can also be variables which have not been manipulated, such as gender, age, ethnic origin, and social class. Because they cannot be separated from the individual who has them, they are sometimes referred to as *subject* variables. A study which investigated the effect of such subject variables would also be called a factorial design.

One of the main advantages of factorial designs, other than the study of interaction effects, is that they generally provide a more sensitive or powerful statistical test of the effect of the factors than designs which investigate just one factor at a time. To understand why this is the case, it is necessary to describe how a one-way and a two-way (that is, a factorial) analysis of variance differ. In one-way analysis of variance, the variance in the means of the groups (or levels) is compared with the variance within them combined for all the groups:

$$F = \frac{\text{variance between groups}}{\text{variance within groups}}$$

The between-groups variance is calculated by comparing the group mean with the overall or grand mean, while the within-groups variance is worked out by comparing the individual scores in the group with its mean. If the group means differ, then their variance should be greater than the average of those within them. This situation is illustrated in Figure 9.4 where the means of the three groups (M_1, M_2 and M_3) are quite widely separated, causing a greater spread of between-groups variance (V_B) while the variance within the groups (V_1, V_2 and V_3) is considerably less when combined (V_W).

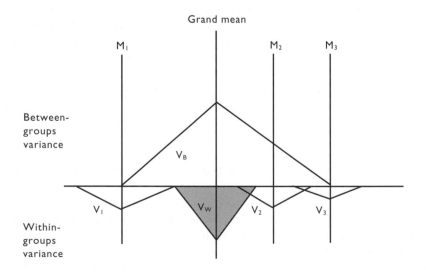

Figure 9.4 Schematic representation of a significant one-way effect

Now the variance within the groups is normally thought of as error since this is the only way in which we can estimate it, while the between-groups variance is considered to consist of this error plus the effect of the factor which is being investigated. While some of the within-groups variance may be due to error, such as that of measurement and of procedure, the rest of it will be due to factors which we have not controlled, such as gender, age and motivation. In other words, the within-groups variance will contain error as well as variance due to other factors, and so will be larger than if it just contained error variance. Consequently, it will provide an overestimate of error. In a two-factor design, on the other hand, the variance due to the other factor can be removed from this overestimate of the error variance, thereby giving a more accurate calculation of it. If, for example, we had just compared the effectiveness of the drug treatment with psychotherapy in reducing depression, then some of the within-groups variance would have been due to gender but treated as error, and may have obscured any differential effect due to treatment.

Covariate design

Another way of reducing error variance is by removing the influence of a non-categorical variable (that is, one which is not nominal) which we believe to be biasing the results. This is particularly useful in designs where participants are not randomly assigned to factors, such as in the Job Survey study, or where random assignment did not result in the groups being equal in terms of some other important variable, such as how depressed patients were before being treated. A covariate is a variable which is linearly related to the one we are most directly interested in, usually called the *dependent* or *criterion* variable.

We shall give two examples of the way in which the effect of covariates may be controlled. Suppose, for instance, we wanted to find out the relationship between job satisfaction and the two factors of gender and ethnic group in the Job Survey data and we knew that job satisfaction was positively correlated with income, so that people who were earning more were also more satisfied with their jobs. It is possible that both gender and ethnic group will also be related to income. Women may earn less than men and non-white workers may earn less than their white counterparts. If so, then the relationship of these two factors to job satisfaction is likely to be biased by their association with income. To control for this, we shall remove the influence of income by covarying it out. In this case, income is the co-variate. If income were not correlated with job satisfaction, then there would be no need to do this. Consequently, it is only advisable to control a covariate when it has been found to be related to the dependent variable.

In true experimental designs, we try to control the effect of variables other than the independent ones by randomly assigning participants to different treatments or conditions. However, when the number of participants allocated to treatments is small (say, about ten or less), there is a stronger possibility that there will be chance differences between them. If, for example, we are interested in comparing the

Table 9.1 The Depression Project data

Id	Treat	Gender	Age	Patpre	Infpre	Patpost	Infpost
01	1	1	27	25	27	20	19
02	1	2	30	29	26	25	27
03	1	1	33	26	25	23	26
04	1	2	36	31	33	24	26
05	1	1	41	33	30	29	28
06	1	2	44	28	30	23	26
07	1	1	47	34	30	30	31
08	1	2	51	35	37	29	28
09	2	1	25	21	24	9	15
10	2	2	27	20	21	9	12
11	2	1	30	23	20	10	8
12	2	2	31	22	28	14	18
13	2	1	33	25	22	15	17
14	2	2	34	26	23	17	16
15	2	1	35	24	26	9	13
16	2	2	37	27	25	18	20
17	2	1	38	25	21	11	8
18	2	2	42	29	30	19	21
19	3	1	30	34	37	23	25
20	3	2	33	31	27	15	13
21	3	1	36	32	35	20	21
22	3	2	37	33	35	20	18
23	3	1	39	40	38	33	35
24	3	2	41	34	31	18	19
25	3	1	42	34	36	23	27
26	3	2	44	37	31	14	11
27	3	1	45	36	38	24	25
28	3	2	47	38	35	25	27
29	3	1	48	37	39	29	28
30	3	2	50	39	37	23	24

MULTIVARIATE ANALYSIS

The example we have given is the more common one in which there are unequal numbers of cases on one or more of the factors. Although it is possible to equalise them by randomly omitting two participants from the psychotherapy treatment and four from the drug one, this would be a waste of valuable data and so is not recommended.

There are four main ways of analysing the results of factorial designs with SPSS. The first method, referred to as *Type I* in SPSS and previously known as the *hierarchical* or *sequential* approach, allows the investigator to determine the order of the effects. If one factor is thought to precede another, then it can be placed first. This approach should be used in non-experimental designs where the factors can be ordered in some sequential manner. If, for example, we are interested in the effect of ethnic group and income on job satisfaction, then ethnic group would be entered first since income cannot determine the ethnic group to which we belong.

Type II, previously known as *classic experimental* or *least squares* approach, can be used with balanced or unbalanced designs where there are some cases in all cells. Tabachnick and Fidell (1996) recommend that this method should be used for non-experimental designs where there are unequal numbers of cases in cells and where cells having larger numbers of cases are thought to be more important.

Type III, previously known as the *regression, unweighted means* or *unique* approach, is used where there are an equal number of cases in each cell or where the design is balanced in that the cell frequencies are proportional in terms of their marginal distributions. Tabachnick and Fidell (1996) recommend that this method should also be used for true experimental designs where there are unequal numbers of cases in cells due to random drop-out and where all cells are considered to be equally important.

Type IV is applied with balanced or unbalanced designs where there are no cases in some cells.

All four methods produce the same result for analysis of variance designs when there are equal numbers of participants in cells. For an unbalanced two-way analysis of variance design they only differ in the way they handle main effects so the results for the interaction effects and the error are the same. Where the main effects are not independent, the component sums of squares do not add up to the total sum of squares.

In this chapter, we have followed the recommendation of Tabachnick and Fidell (1996) in using the Type II method for true experimental designs.

Factorial design

To determine the effect of treatment, gender and their interaction on post-test depression as seen by the patient, the following procedure is needed:

→**Analyze** →**General Linear Model** →**Univariate...** [opens **Univariate** dialog box shown in Box 9.1]
→**patpost** →▶ button beside **Dependent Variable:** [puts **patpost** in this box]
→**gender** →▶ button beside **Fixed Factor[s]:** [puts **gender** in this box] →**treat** →▶ button beside **Fixed Factor[s]:** [puts **treat** in this box]
→**Options...** [opens **Univariate: Options** subdialog box shown in Box 9.2]
→**Descriptive statistics** →**Homogeneity tests** →**Continue** [closes **Univariate: Options** subdialog box]
→**Plots...** [opens **Univariate: Profile Plots** subdialog box shown in Box 9.3]
→**gender** →▶ button beside **Horizontal Axis:** [puts **gender** in this box] →**treat** →▶ button beside **Separate Lines:** [puts **treat** in this box] →**Add** [puts **gender*treat** in box under **Plots:**] →**Continue** [closes **Univariate: Profile Plots** subdialog box]
→**OK**

Table 9.2 Means of post-test depression (**patpost**) in the three
treatments for men and women (Depression Project)

Descriptive Statistics

Dependent Variable: PATPOST

GENDER	TREAT	Mean	Std. Deviation	N
1	1	25.50	4.80	4
	2	10.80	2.49	5
	3	25.33	4.76	6
	Total	20.53	8.10	15
2	1	25.25	2.63	4
	2	15.40	4.04	5
	3	19.17	4.36	6
	Total	19.53	5.33	15
Total	1	25.38	3.58	8
	2	13.10	3.98	10
	3	22.25	5.41	12
	Total	20.03	6.75	30

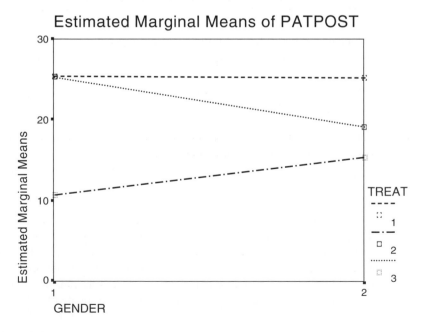

Figure 9.5 Post-test patient depression of men and women
(Depression Project)

Table 9.3 **Homogeneity tests** output
(Depression Project)

Levene's Test of Equality of Error Variance[a]s

Dependent Variable: PATPOST

F	df1	df2	Sig.
1.213	5	24	.333

Tests the null hypothesis that the error variance of the
dependent variable is equal across groups.

a. Design: Intercept+GENDER+TREAT+GENDER
   *TREAT

Table 9.4 Tests of significance for main and interaction effects in an unrelated
factorial design (Depression Project)

Tests of Between-Subjects Effects

Dependent Variable: PATPOST

Source	Type III Sum of Squares	df	Mean Square	F	Sig.
Corrected Model	935.050[a]	5	187.010	11.570	.000
Intercept	11959.543	1	11959.543	739.924	.000
GENDER	2.676	1	2.676	.166	.688
TREAT	767.942	2	383.971	23.756	.000
GENDER * TREAT	159.608	2	79.804	4.937	.016
Error	387.917	24	16.163		
Total	13363.000	30			
Corrected Total	1322.967	29			

a. R Squared = .707 (Adjusted R Squared = .646)

Having found that there is an overall significant difference in depression for the
three treatments, we need to determine where this difference lies. One way of
doing this is to test for differences between two treatments at a time. If we had not
anticipated certain differences between treatments, we would apply post hoc tests
such as Scheffé to determine their statistical significance, whereas if we had
predicted them we would use unrelated t tests (see Chapter 7).

Table 9.6 Analysis of covariance table showing test of homogeneity of slope of regression line within cells (Depression Project)

Tests of Between-Subjects Effects

Dependent Variable: PATPOST

Source	Type III Sum of Squares	df	Mean Square	F	Sig.
Corrected Model	1071.498[a]	5	214.300	20.453	.000
Intercept	43.642	1	43.642	4.165	.052
TREAT	16.905	2	8.453	.807	.458
PATPRE	299.436	1	299.436	28.578	.000
TREAT * PATPRE	4.907	2	2.454	.234	.793
Error	251.468	24	10.478		
Total	13363.000	30			
Corrected Total	1322.967	29			

a. R Squared = .810 (Adjusted R Squared = .770)

→**Custom** →**treat** →▶ button [puts **treat** under **Model:**] →**patpre** →▶ button [puts **patpre** under **Model:**] →**Interaction** →**treat** →**patpre** →▶ button [puts **treat*patpre** under **Model:**] →**Continue** [closes **Univariate: Model** subdialog box]
→**OK**

The output for this procedure is presented in Table 9.6. The interaction between the independent variable of treatment and the covariate of **patpre** is not significant since *p* is 0.793. This means that the slope of the regression line in each of the cells is similar and therefore the second assumption is met.

Consequently we can proceed with the main analysis of covariance using the following procedure:

→**Analyze** →**General Linear Model** →**Univariate…** [opens **Univariate** dialog box shown in Box 9.1]
→**patpost** →▶ button beside **Dependent Variable:** [puts **patpost** in this box]
→**treat** →▶ button beside **Fixed Factor[s]:** [puts **treat** in this box] →**patpre** →▶ button beside **Covariate[s]:** [puts **patpre** in this box]
→**Model…** [opens **Univariate: Model** subdialog box shown in Box 9.4]
→**Full factorial** →**Continue** [closes **Univariate: Model** subdialog box]
→**Options…** [opens **Univariate: Options** subdialog box shown in Box 9.2]
→**treat** →▶ button [puts **treat** under **Display Means for:**] →**Continue** [closes **Univariate: Options** subdialog box]
→**OK**

The analysis of covariance table in Table 9.7 shows that the relationship

Table 9.7 Analysis of covariance table (Depression Project)

Tests of Between-Subjects Effects

Dependent Variable: PATPOST

Source	Type III Sum of Squares	df	Mean Square	F	Sig.
Corrected Model	1066.591[a]	3	355.530	36.056	.000
Intercept	41.426	1	41.426	4.201	.051
PATPRE	298.650	1	298.650	30.287	.000
TREAT	339.161	2	169.580	17.198	.000
Error	256.375	26	9.861		
Total	13363.000	30			
Corrected Total	1322.967	29			

a. R Squared = .806 (Adjusted R Squared = .784)

between the covariate (**patpre**) and the dependent variable (**patpost**) is significant. Consequently, it is appropriate to proceed with the interpretation of the covariate analysis. This table also shows there is a significant treatment effect when pre-treatment depression is covaried out.

An inspection of the adjusted means for the three treatments presented in Table 9.8 with the observed means in Table 9.2 shows that controlling for pre-treatment depression has little effect on the mean for the control group, which remains at about 25. However, it makes a considerable difference to the means of the two treatment conditions, reversing their order so that patients who received psycho-therapy report themselves as being more depressed than those given the drug treatment. The means have been adjusted using the weighted rather than the unweighted covariate grand mean (Cramer, 1998). The Bryant–Paulson post hoc test for determining whether this difference is significant is described in Stevens (1996).

Table 9.8 Adjusted means of post-test depression in the three treatments (Depression Project)

TREAT

Dependent Variable: PATPOST

TREAT	Mean	Std. Error	95% Confidence Interval	
			Lower Bound	Upper Bound
1	25.528[a]	1.111	23.245	27.811
2	19.660[a]	1.551	16.471	22.849
3	16.681[a]	1.359	13.888	19.474

a. Evaluated at covariates appeared in the model: PATPRE = 30.27

Table 9.9 Means and standard deviations of post-test depression scores for patients (**patpost**) and informants (**infpost**) for the three treatments (Depression Project)

Descriptive Statistics

	TREAT	Mean	Std. Deviation	N
PATPOST	1	25.38	3.58	8
	2	13.10	3.98	10
	3	22.25	5.41	12
	Total	20.03	6.75	30
INFPOST	1	26.38	3.42	8
	2	14.80	4.54	10
	3	22.75	6.73	12
	Total	21.07	6.99	30

Table 9.10 Box's M test (Depression Project)

Box's Test of Equality of Covariance Matrice[a]s

Box's M	7.985
F	1.182
df1	6
df2	9324.416
Sig.	.313

Tests the null hypothesis that the observed covariance matrices of the dependent variables are equal across groups.

a. Design: Intercept+TREAT

Table 9.11 Levene's test (Depression Project)

Levene's Test of Equality of Error Variance[a]s

	F	df1	df2	Sig.
PATPOST	.456	2	27	.638
INFPOST	2.540	2	27	.098

Tests the null hypothesis that the error variance of the dependent variable is equal across groups.

a. Design: Intercept+TREAT

Table 9.12 Bartlett's test of sphericity
(Depression Project)

Bartlett's Test of Sphericity[a]

Likelihood Ratio	.000
Approx. Chi-Square	44.656
df	2
Sig.	.000

Tests the null hypothesis that the residual covariance
matrix is proportional to an identity matrix.

a. Design: Intercept+TREAT

Table 9.13 Multivariate tests of significance for the treatment effect
(Depression Project)

Multivariate Tests[c]

Effect		Value	F	Hypothesis df	Error df	Sig.
Intercept	Pillai's Trace	.956	280.195[a]	2.000	26.000	.000
	Wilks' Lambda	.044	280.195[a]	2.000	26.000	.000
	Hotelling's Trace	21.553	280.195[a]	2.000	26.000	.000
	Roy's Largest Root	21.553	280.195[a]	2.000	26.000	.000
TREAT	Pillai's Trace	.618	6.032	4.000	54.000	.000
	Wilks' Lambda	.393	7.724[a]	4.000	52.000	.000
	Hotelling's Trace	1.513	9.456	4.000	50.000	.000
	Roy's Largest Root	1.494	20.169[b]	2.000	27.000	.000

a. Exact statistic
b. The statistic is an upper bound on F that yields a lower bound on the significance level.
c. Design: Intercept+TREAT

appropriate to use the multivariate test of significance to determine whether there are significant differences between the treatments. The result of this test is presented in Table 9.13 and shows the treatment effect to be significant when the two measures are taken together.

The univariate F tests for the treatment effect, which are presented in Table 9.14, show that the treatments differ on both the dependent measures when they are analysed separately. To determine which treatments differ significantly from one another, it would be necessary to carry out a series of unrelated t tests or post hoc tests as discussed previously.

Variables [time]: [puts **infpost** in this box] →**treat** →▶ button beside **Between-Subjects Factor[s]:** [puts **treat** in this box] →**gender** →▶ button beside **Between-Subjects Factor[s]:** [puts **gender** in this box] →**age** →▶ button beside **Covariate(s):** [puts **age** in this box]
→**Options…** [opens **Repeated Measures: Options** subdialog box shown in Box 9.9]
→**Descriptive statistics** →**Transformation matrix** →**Continue** [closes **Repeated Measures: Options** subdialog box]
→**OK**

In conducting a multivariate analysis of covariance, it is necessary to check that the covariate (**age**) is significantly correlated with the two dependent variables, which it is as the output in Table 9.17 shows.

The output for the multivariate tests is reproduced in Table 9.18. This shows a significant effect for the time by treatment by gender interaction effect.

The univariate tests in Table 9.19 demonstrate the interaction effect to be significant ($p < 0.0005$) for the patient measure only (**pat**). It is not significant ($p = 0.176$) for the informant measure (**inf**). **Pat** refers to the transformed score which is the difference between the patient's pre- and post-test measures as can be seen in Table 9.20. **Inf** represents the difference between the informant's pre- and post-test scores. To interpret these results, it would be necessary to compute the mean pre- and post-treatment patient depression scores, adjusted for age, for men and women in the three treatments. Additional analyses would have to be conducted to test these interpretations, as described previously.

Table 9.17 Relationship between the covariate of age and the two transformed variables (Depression Project)

Tests of Between-Subjects Effects

Transformed Variable: Average

Source	Measure	Type III Sum of Squares	df	Mean Square	F	Sig.
Intercept	PAT	200.217	1	200.217	16.471	.000
	INF	322.787	1	322.787	19.914	.000
AGE	PAT	298.580	1	298.580	24.562	.000
	INF	192.043	1	192.043	11.848	.002
TREAT	PAT	549.908	2	274.954	22.619	.000
	INF	531.276	2	265.638	16.389	.000
GENDER	PAT	9.063	1	9.063	.746	.397
	INF	8.461	1	8.461	.522	.477
TREAT * GENDER	PAT	100.978	2	50.489	4.153	.029
	INF	324.974	2	162.487	10.025	.001
Error	PAT	279.587	23	12.156		
	INF	372.799	23	16.209		

Table 9.18 Multivariate tests for the interaction between time, treatment and gender (Depression Project)

Multivariate[c,d]

Within Subjects Effect		Value	F	Hypothesis df	Error df	Sig.
TIME	Pillai's Trace	.364	6.305[a]	2.000	22.000	.007
	Wilks' Lambda	.636	6.305[a]	2.000	22.000	.007
	Hotelling's Trace	.573	6.305[a]	2.000	22.000	.007
	Roy's Largest Root	.573	6.305[a]	2.000	22.000	.007
TIME * AGE	Pillai's Trace	.009	.097[a]	2.000	22.000	.908
	Wilks' Lambda	.991	.097[a]	2.000	22.000	.908
	Hotelling's Trace	.009	.097[a]	2.000	22.000	.908
	Roy's Largest Root	.009	.097[a]	2.000	22.000	.908
TIME * TREAT	Pillai's Trace	.781	7.364	4.000	46.000	.000
	Wilks' Lambda	.241	11.423[a]	4.000	44.000	.000
	Hotelling's Trace	3.066	16.099	4.000	42.000	.000
	Roy's Largest Root	3.037	34.927[b]	2.000	23.000	.000
TIME * GENDER	Pillai's Trace	.098	1.196[a]	2.000	22.000	.321
	Wilks' Lambda	.902	1.196[a]	2.000	22.000	.321
	Hotelling's Trace	.109	1.196[a]	2.000	22.000	.321
	Roy's Largest Root	.109	1.196[a]	2.000	22.000	.321
TIME * TREAT * GENDER	Pillai's Trace	.576	4.653	4.000	46.000	.003
	Wilks' Lambda	.439	5.606[a]	4.000	44.000	.001
	Hotelling's Trace	1.245	6.537	4.000	42.000	.000
	Roy's Largest Root	1.217	13.998[b]	2.000	23.000	.000

a. Exact statistic
b. The statistic is an upper bound on F that yields a lower bound on the significance level.
c.
   Design: Intercept+AGE+TREAT+GENDER+TREAT * GENDER
   Within Subjects Design: TIME
d. Tests are based on averaged variables.

Table 9.19 Univariate tests for the interaction effect between time, treatment and gender (Depression Project)

Tests of Within-Subjects Contrasts

Source	Measure	TIME	Type III Sum of Squares	df	Mean Square	F	Sig.
TIME	PAT	Linear	32.706	1	32.706	12.916	.002
	INF	Linear	31.259	1	31.259	4.244	.051
TIME * AGE	PAT	Linear	9.094E-02	1	9.094E-02	.036	.851
	INF	Linear	.218	1	.218	.030	.865
TIME * TREAT	PAT	Linear	174.857	2	87.428	34.526	.000
	INF	Linear	185.773	2	92.886	12.610	.000
TIME * GENDER	PAT	Linear	6.274	1	6.274	2.478	.129
	INF	Linear	6.758	1	6.758	.917	.348
TIME * TREAT * GENDER	PAT	Linear	60.289	2	30.144	11.904	.000
	INF	Linear	27.641	2	13.820	1.876	.176
Error(TIME)	PAT	Linear	58.242	23	2.532		
	INF	Linear	169.423	23	7.366		

Table 9.20 Transformed variables (Depression Project)

Average

Transformed Variable: AVERAGE

Dependent Variable	Measure	
	PAT	INF
PATPRE	.707	.000
PATPOST	.707	.000
INFPRE	.000	.707
INFPOST	.000	.707

EXERCISES

1   What are the two main advantages in studying the effects of two independent variables rather than one?
2   What is meant when two variables are said to interact?
3   How would you determine whether there was a significant interaction between two independent variables?
4   A colleague is interested in the relationship between alcohol, anxiety and gender on performance. Participants are randomly assigned to receiving one of four increasing dosages of alcohol. In addition, they are divided into three groups of low, moderate and high anxiety. Which is the dependent variable?
5   How many factors are there in this design?
6   How many levels of anxiety are there?
7   How would you describe this design?
8   If there are unequal numbers of participants in each group and if the variable names for alcohol, anxiety, gender and performance are **alcohol**, **anxiety**, **gender** and **perform** respectively, what is the appropriate SPSS procedure for examining the effect of the first three variables on performance?
9   You are interested in examining the effect of three different methods of teaching on learning to read. Although participants have been randomly assigned to the three methods, you think that differences in intelligence may obscure any effects. How would you try to control statistically for the effects of intelligence?
10   What is the appropriate SPSS procedure for examining the effect of three teaching methods on learning to read, covarying out the effect of intelligence when the names for these three variables are **methods**, **read** and **intell** respectively?
11   You are studying what effect physical attractiveness has on judgements of intelligence, likeability, honesty and self-confidence. Participants are shown a photograph of either an attractive or an unattractive person and are asked

to judge the extent to which this person has these four characteristics. How would you describe the design of this study?

12   If the names of the five variables in this study are **attract, intell, likeable, honesty** and **confid** respectively, what is the appropriate SPSS procedure you would use to analyse the results of this study?

Chapter 10

Multivariate analysis

Exploring relationships among three or more variables

In this chapter we shall be concerned with a variety of approaches to the examination of relationships when more than two variables are involved. Clearly, these concerns follow on directly from those of Chapter 8, in which we focused upon bivariate analysis of relationships. In the present chapter, we shall be concerned to explore the reasons for wanting to analyse three or more variables in conjunction; that is, why multivariate analysis is an important aspect of the examination of relationships among variables.

The basic rationale for multivariate analysis is to allow the researcher to discount the alternative explanations of a relationship that can arise when a survey/correlational design has been employed. The experimental researcher can discount alternative explanations of a relationship through the combination of having a control group as well as an experimental group (or through a number of experimental groups) and random assignment (see Chapter 1). The absence of these characteristics, which in large part derives from the failure or inability to manipulate the independent variable in a survey/correlational study, means that a number of potentially confounding factors may exist. For example, we may find a relationship between people's self-assigned social class (whether they describe themselves as middle or working class) and their voting preference (Conservative or Labour). But there are a number of problems that can be identified with interpreting such a relationship as causal. Might the relationship be spurious? This possibility could arise because people on higher incomes are both more likely to consider themselves middle class and to vote Conservative. Also, even if the relationship is not spurious, does the relationship apply equally to young and old? We know that age affects voting preferences, so how does this variable interact with self-assigned social class in regard to voting behaviour? Such a finding would imply that the class–voting relationship is moderated by age. The problem of spuriousness arises because we cannot make some people think they are middle class and others working class and then randomly assign subjects to the two categories. If we wanted to carry out an experimental study to establish whether a moderated relationship exists whereby age moderates the class–voting relationship, we would use a factorial design (see Chapter 9). Obviously, we are not able to create such experimental conditions, so